PARLIAMENTARY SUPREMACY AND JUDICIAL INDEPENDENCE:

A COMMONWEALTH APPROACH

Proceedings of the Latimer House
Joint Colloquium, June 1998

Edited by
John Hatchard
General Secretary, Commonwealth Legal
Education Association
and
Peter Slinn
Vice President, Commonwealth Legal
Education Association

Cavendish
Publishing
Limited

London • Sydney

First published in Great Britain 1999 by Cavendish Publishing Limited, The Glass House, Wharton Street, London WC1X 9PX, United Kingdom

Telephone: + 44 (0) 171 278 8000   Facsimile: + 44 (0) 171 278 8080

E-mail: info@cavendishpublishing.com

Visit our Home Page on http://www.cavendishpublishing.com

British Library Cataloguing in Publication Data. A catalogue record for this book is available from the British Library.

ISBN 1 85941 523 7

GIFT

Printed and bound in Great Britain

PREFACE

A Joint Colloquium on *Parliamentary Supremacy and Judicial Independence ... Towards a Commonwealth Model* was held at Latimer House in the United Kingdom, from 15 to 19 June 1998. Over 60 participants attended, representing 20 Commonwealth countries and three overseas territories. This was the first Commonwealth gathering to bring together at senior level parliamentarians, including those holding ministerial office, with judges, legal practitioners and legal academics. The objective was to promote a dialogue between those at the cutting edge of good governance issues with the specific aim of drafting guidelines as to best practice with regard to relations between the executive, parliament and the judiciary in the context of the Harare and Millbrook commitments.

That objective was achieved during three days and nights of intensive discussion. The Guidelines reproduced herein are not intended to be yet another high-sounding declaration of good intentions but an operational manual of good practice which can be considered for implementation in every Commonwealth jurisdiction. The principles outlined in the Guidelines have been supported by the member associations concerned in their dealings with each other.

Accordingly, they will be submitted for consideration to the Commonwealth Law Ministers at their Meeting in May 1999 and, thence, to the Commonwealth Heads of Government Meeting. Thus, the Guidelines could form an integral part of Commonwealth processes for monitoring compliance with the Harare Principles.

In addition, a judge, parliamentarian or legal practitioner or any other member of civil society faced with a breach of the Guidelines will be able to invoke them against abuses.

The Guidelines themselves are set out on page 17 below, as drafted by the participants during the Colloquium.

The Colloquium was sponsored by the Commonwealth Lawyers' Association, the Commonwealth Legal Education Association, the Commonwealth Magistrates' and Judges' Association and the Commonwealth Parliamentary Association. The gathering would not have been possible without the generous financial support of the Commonwealth Foundation, the Commonwealth Secretariat and the United Kingdom Foreign and Commonwealth Office. The sponsoring Associations would also like to record their deep appreciation of the tireless efforts of Shem Baldeosingh, Karen Brewer, Meenakshi Dhar, Art Donahoe, John Hatchard, Michael Lambert, Helen Potts (nee Ramsey) and Peter Slinn in providing the ad hoc secretariat.

London
March 1999

CONTENTS

Contents

CHAPTER 1

REPORT OF THE CONFERENCE PROCEEDINGS

Peter Slinn

INTRODUCTION

The genesis of the Joint Colloquium lay in the shared concern of a number of Commonwealth organisations about the effective implementation of the good governance, democracy and human rights agenda embodied in the Harare Declaration. These matters were of particular concern to the sponsoring organisations as being representative of those professions directly involved in the processes whereby these benefits are secured or imperilled – judges (the CMJA), parliamentarians (the CPA), practising lawyers (the CLA) and legal educators (the CLEA).

The Commonwealth has acted at inter-governmental level to promote and secure the Harare Principles, most notably through the Millbrook Commonwealth Action Programme including the establishment of the Commonwealth Ministerial Action Group (CMAG) and through the work of the Commonwealth Secretariat.[1] Specific initiatives have included the convening, under the aegis of the Secretariat, of a working group on the independence of the judiciary due to report in 1999. Training programmes on good governance, administrative law and human rights have continued under the direction of the Legal and Constitutional Affairs Division of the Secretariat.[2]

Parliamentarians and all three branches of the legal profession have been directly concerned with the promotion and fulfilment of the Harare commitments.[3] The CMJA has run training seminars on human rights themes and is developing a code of judicial ethics;[4] the CPA has conducted training seminars for parliamentarians with particular emphasis on the needs of

---

1   Report of the Commonwealth Secretary General, 1997, pp 20–21.

2   See, in particular, the 'Bangalore' series of judicial colloquia and *Good Government and Administrative Law*, Commonwealth Secretariat, 1996.

3   This is reflected in the objectives of the four sponsoring organisations, including pursuit of the positive ideals of parliamentary democracy (CPA), promoting high standard of legal education (CLEA), the maintenance and promotion of the rule of law throughout the Commonwealth by ensuring that the people of the Commonwealth are served by an independent and efficient legal profession (CLA) and to advance the administration of law by promoting the independence of the judiciary (CMJA).

4   Report of the Eleventh Triennal Conference, Cape Town, 25 October–1 November 1997.

transitional democracies; the CLA has provided training seminars for developing Commonwealth practitioners; and the CLEA is developing model curricula to facilitate the teaching of human rights and rule of law issues to the next generation. The CLA, CPA and CLEA have also sponsored the Commonwealth Human Rights Initiative (CHRI) which has been directly involved in monitoring Commonwealth countries where abuse of the Harare Principles has been threatened or has occurred, including sending missions to Nigeria and to Zambia.[5]

In the light of all this experience, the sponsoring organisations identified a need for a quite new kind of Commonwealth gathering, building on existing discrete initiatives of the type referred to above, but quite distinct from training workshops, academic conferences and deliberations within the confines of each professional cadre. The idea was to bring together for the first time at senior level, parliamentarians, including those holding ministerial office, with judges, legal practitioners and legal academicians with the object not only of promoting a dialogue between those at the cutting edge of good governance issues but with the specific aim of drafting guidelines as to best practice with regard to relations between the executive, parliament and the judiciary in the context of the Harare and Millbrook commitments. That objective was achieved during three days and nights of intensive discussion. The Guidelines reproduced herein are not intended to be yet another high-sounding declaration of good intentions but an operational manual of good practice capable of implementation in every Commonwealth jurisdiction. The principles outlined in the Guidelines have been supported by the member associations concerned in their dealings with each other. Also, they will be submitted for consideration by Commonwealth Law Ministers at their May 1999 meeting and following that to the Commonwealth Heads of Government Meeting. Thus, the Guidelines could play a formal part in the process of implementation and of monitoring compliance with the Harare Principles. In this way, a judge, parliamentarian or legal practitioner or any other member of civil society faced with a breach of the Guidelines will be able to invoke them 'horizontally' against another professional or 'vertically' against abuse by governmental or other authority. All Commonwealth governments and relevant elements in civil society will be asked to accept a monitoring procedure as indicated in paragraph IX of the Guidelines which would include the power to solicit reports on compliance from each Commonwealth member. It would be possible to utilise the existing CMAG machinery by expanding its remit to include the monitoring of compliance with the Guidelines. CMAG's findings, which would be based on reports from each Commonwealth member and on submissions through the sponsoring

---

5   Sadly, there is no reason to change the verdict of the CHRI Advisory Group, *Put Our World to Rights*, in August 1991: 'On the whole, [the Commonwealth's] members' record on human rights is poor', p 6.

organisations, would then be considered as a regular part of the CHOGM agenda. This process would eliminate a major weakness of the current Millbrook Programme of Action, which so far has limited itself to 'dealing with serious and persistent violations' of the Harare Principles, in effect confining CMAG's remit to Commonwealth countries which were then under military rule.

The Latimer House system as proposed is designed to provide positive support for the achievement and maintenance of good practice in implementing the Harare Declaration. However, there is overwhelming evidence of breaches of the Harare Principles in many Commonwealth jurisdictions which ostensibly maintain a democratic system under the rule of law.[6] This system will also empower principal elements of civil society in all Commonwealth countries to participate in the compliance process.

The sponsoring organisations will only have realised their aim if the Guidelines become a living instrument of good governance and the rule of law and a fresh blueprint for the realisation of the ideals of the modern Commonwealth.

THE STRUCTURE OF THE COLLOQUIUM

The meeting was structured so as to ensure an informed analysis of what were perceived to be the core issues at stake in achieving satisfactory and balanced relationships between the executive, parliament and the judiciary.[7] The first plenary session examined ways of protecting judicial and parliamentary independence; plenaries two and three examined relations between parliament and the judiciary; plenary four reviewed the role of non-judicial and non-parliamentary institutions such as the practising legal profession and national human rights institutions; plenary five scrutinised the delicate relations between the executive and the parliamentary and judicial arms; and plenary six looked at the role of civil society, the perceptions of the public at large and the vital role of the media in ensuring transparency. The plenary sessions were supported by a series of workshops which reviewed sections of the draft guidelines that were adopted in plenary at the conclusion of the Colloquium. The Guidelines are therefore the product of a genuinely participatory process involving an emerging consensus harmonising the differing concerns of judges, parliamentarians and ministers. Thus, the colloquium was in marked contrast to international gatherings where the final

---

6   However, in the year following the Edinburgh Declaration, no situations in other Commonwealth countries were brought to the attention of CMAG as envisaged by paragraph 20 of the Edinburgh Communiqué.

7   The list of participants is found in Appendix 3.

communiqué exists in draft form in advance and the actual input of delegates is in practice severely restricted.[8]

SUMMARY OF DISCUSSIONS

The keynote address was delivered by Lord Irvine of Lairg, Lord High Chancellor of Great Britain.[9] In the course of his speech, he defended the British practice of using judges to conduct inquiries into matters of the highest political sensitivity. However, he also staunchly defended the British application of the doctrine of separation of powers in the context of parliamentary sovereignty:

> There is no question of our judges misusing the opportunities presented by judicial review in an attempt to establish themselves as a power to rival the sovereignty of parliament. In the United Kingdom, the executive, legislative and judicial branches of government are not equal and co-ordinate. Parliament is the senior partner.[10]

This position would not be changed fundamentally by the coming into force of the Human Rights Act.[11] The lack of any jurisdiction to strike down incompatible primary legislation would not generally impair the ability of courts to ensure the protection of human rights. Noting that the position in the United Kingdom differed from that in the United States and Canada,[12] Lord Irvine observed that each country must find a solution which is sensitive to its domestic culture, achieving an effective balance between the powers of the judges and the powers of government and parliament.[13] This indeed neatly summed up the ambitious task which the sponsors of the colloquium had set the assembled delegates.

In discussion following the Lord Chancellor's address, speakers from a wide range of jurisdictions emphasised the limitations on the doctrine of parliamentary sovereignty, which in developing Commonwealth countries was said to mask the reality of executive power. Parliament was often marginalised and its proceedings ill reported and seen as remote from the people. The Lord Chancellor's elevation of parliament as the 'senior partner'

---

8   This meant that the midnight oil was burnt throughout the colloquium and tribute should be paid to the heroic staff of the sponsoring organisations. They made possible the continuous drafting process, without the logistical support that other high-level international conferences normally enjoy.

9   Below, p 29.

10 Below, p 31.

11 At the time of Lord Irvine's address, the Bill was in the committee stage in the House of Commons. It received the Royal Assent in November 1998, but will not come into force until 2000.

12 And many other Commonwealth countries represented at the Colloquium.

13 Below, p 33.

was criticised on the basis that the relationship between the executive, judiciary and parliament was that of an equilateral not an isosceles triangle. Indeed, judges might be called upon to make difficult decisions which a popularly elected legislature might be reluctant to make.

PLENARY 1
PRESERVING JUDICIAL AND PARLIAMENTARY INDEPENDENCE

The first plenary session, chaired by Mr Rodney Hansen, QC (New Zealand, CLA), was addressed by Professor James Read (United Kingdom, CLEA),[14] The Hon Justice Dame Silvia Cartwright (New Zealand, CMJA),[15] The Hon Chief Justice Anthony Gubbay (Zimbabwe, CMJA),[16] and Ms Susan Barnes, MP (Canada, CPA).

In providing an overview of the respective roles of parliament and the judiciary, Professor Read reminded participants that throughout the Commonwealth these institutions were established by written constitutions which were subject to judicial interpretation. Even in the United Kingdom, current changes amounted to the creation of a constitutional edifice expanding the judicial role. Devolution of government, the Human Rights Act and the subjection of the 'sovereign' parliament to the institutions of the European Union now gave British judges for the first time power to examine the validity of Acts of parliament. The 'Westminster Model' of government, still dominant in the Commonwealth, denied the 'separation of powers', being based upon the close integration of legislature and executive. Thus, in the United Kingdom the Lord Chancellor himself was at the apex of the executive, legislative and judicial authority. The essential separation of powers was seen in the independence of the judiciary, which required constant re-assertion in terms of selection, appointment and tenure, provision of resources, accessibility and consequent authority. The freedom of parliament, including that of individual members, was significant but in many states parliaments were weak, lacking the resources adequately to enforce government accountability.

Dame Silvia Cartwright drew attention to the pressures to which judicial independence was subjected, not only from governmental and parliamentary organs but also from media lobby groups and public prejudices. However,

---

14 'The Constitution, Parliament and the Courts', below, p 35.
15 'The Judiciary: Qualifications, Training and Gender Balance', below, p 39.
16 'The Independence of the Judiciary with special reference to parliamentary control of tenure, terms and conditions of service and remuneration of judges, judicial autonomy and budgetary control and administration', below, p 47.

judicial independence was essential not for the benefit of judges themselves but for the community as a whole. Qualification and training of judges must be designed to remove gender imbalance and other obstacles to social awareness and the elimination of bigotry and prejudice.

Chief Justice Gubbay sketched the qualities required of a judge to perform his or her task:

> It demands wisdom as well as knowledge, conscience as well as insight, a sense of balance and proportion ...

These qualities would be imperilled by failure to protect judges from political, economic or other influences. The means of such protection included appropriate constitutional provisions relating to appointment and security of tenure, financial independence, and adequate financial resources for judicial purposes, including the ability to travel to consult with judges in other countries:

> The unity of judges in different jurisdictions is most essential for securing the independence of domestic judiciaries.[17]

Merely to lay down principles of judicial independence was not enough. Their implementation required an awareness on the part of society as a whole so that public opinion would be mobilised in defence of judicial independence in the face of any threat from the executive.

From the standpoint of a serving parliamentarian, Ms Barnes admitted that the reputation of parliamentarians had declined owing to failure to maintain links with the people. She reviewed a number of devices affecting the independence of MPs. She was opposed to the system of recall of MPs, which in British Columbia required only a 40% vote on the part of the electorate. She also referred to the role of the caucus, which could play a key role in assuring the responsibility of the executive to members of parliament.

In discussion, reservation was expressed about the role of the caucus as a possible threat to parliamentary supremacy, particularly in states where one party held a dominant position in the legislature. One participant challenged the assumption that the influence of judges on the constitution was inevitably benign by observing that the judiciary itself might constitute a threat to the constitution by usurping the legislative function. One Supreme Court, it was alleged, had taken to redrafting legislation and adopting so pro-active an approach as to amount arguably to an abuse of judicial independence.

There was general agreement that more women judges and more women parliamentarians were needed. For example, very few Commonwealth countries have appointed women judges to their courts of final appeal.[18]

---

17 Below, pp 47, 50.
18 It might be observed that the highest court in the United Kingdom has never had a woman member.

Some subtler threats to the independence and impartiality of judges were discussed, such as the giving of 'plum jobs' to judges on retirement, the anticipation of which might make a judge reluctant to challenge the executive.

PLENARY 2
PARLIAMENT AND THE JUDICIARY I

The second plenary session, chaired by Professor Dawn Oliver (United Kingdom, CLEA), was addressed by Hon Kamla Persad-Bissessar, MP (Trinidad and Tobago, CPA), The Hon Justice Pierré Olivier (South Africa, CMJA),[19] Mr Nana Addo Dankwa Akufo-Addo, MP (Ghana, CPA) and Shri Soli Sorabjee (India, CLA).

Ms Persad-Bissessar, in discussing the law-making process, emphasised the importance of the revising function of a second chamber. Such a chamber was often better equipped than a partisan lower house to give serious consideration to highly technical legislation such as that required to comply with international agreements in the field of world trade.

Judge Olivier's analysis of parliamentary sovereignty and of the judicial role in the law-making process was tempered by the 'horrible' experience of apartheid South Africa. This experience led Judge Olivier to be highly critical of the 'Westminster' model of parliamentary sovereignty, which, however well it might have served Britain, had proved powerless to protect the people of South Africa from unjust laws passed by a parliament which was a rubber stamp of a tyrannical executive:

> ... apartheid could never have come into being without the system of parliamentary sovereignty ...[20]

Judge Olivier painted a vivid picture of the intolerable position in which South African judges were placed in having to apply oppressive laws in relation to which the possibility of judicial review was carefully excluded. Even judicial review of executive action was emasculated by laws conferring specific and draconian powers upon the executive. Judge Olivier contrasted this grim scenario with the situation brought about by the 'miracle of transition' in South Africa. Under the interim and permanent constitutions, judges enjoy powers of judicial review of both executive action and legislation which in the latter case has been used to outlaw the death penalty and the reverse onus of proof in criminal trials. The courts, particularly the new Constitutional Court, have made frequent use of international and comparative precedents:

---

19 'Parliamentary Sovereignty and Judge-Made Law', below, p 53.
20 Below, p 55.

Where judges formerly were reduced to virtually powerless interpreters of rigid apartheid constitutions, they have now achieved their true function and status: they have become co-architects, and not mere bricklayers, of a new and proud society.[21]

Nana Akufo-Addo addressed the basic question of the quality of the law-making process. Can judges and parliamentarians do better? Laws needed to be clear, simple, relevant and consistently applied. In developing countries, parliamentarians found it difficult, in part through lack of resources, to function effectively in improving legislation through committee scrutiny during the passage of Bills. A fresh approach to the interpretation of statutes was required so as to permit reference to parliamentary debates.[22]

He added that another problem faced in many developing countries, including Ghana, was the inaccessibility to much of the population of the official language in which the laws were written. At least 40% of the population could not understand the official language. Nana Akufo-Addo shared Judge Olivier's view of the pernicious impact of the doctrine of parliamentary sovereignty which had also served Ghana ill. However, he was inclined to lay heavy responsibility on the judges themselves, who, even when equipped with full power of review, had failed to use it to limit preventive detention and to strike down other laws affecting individual liberty.[23]

Soli Sorabjee spoke from his perspective as Attorney General of India. Under the Constitution, the Attorney General was independent of government but had the right to address both houses of parliament and their committees. He went on to explain the role of the Attorney General in advising on statutory interpretation, the transference of cases to the Supreme Court and the lodging of contempt petitions (which required the consent of the Attorney General), where there was danger of the misuse of such petitions to shield errant judges. The Attorney General also had an important role in relation to the extensive Indian process of 'public interest litigation' in ensuring that there was a genuine issue to be tried.[24]

In discussion, various issues relating to judicial and parliamentary independence were raised. It was suggested that it was helpful to approach the question of the relationships between the executive, parliament and

---

21 Below, p 57.

22 The approach now adopted in the United Kingdom by the House of Lords in *Pepper v Hart* [1992] 2 WLR 1032; [1993] 1 All ER 1. See, also, p 120, below.

23 He gave as an example the recent decision of the Supreme Court of Ghana (*Republic v Tommy Thompson Books Ltd* [1996–97] Supreme Court of Ghana Law Reports 804), rejecting a challenge to the constitutionality of criminal libel laws.

24 'Public interest litigation' is a remarkable phenomenon of Indian jurisprudence whereby the normal rules of standing are set aside in order to permit access to the courts in the public interest on behalf of disadvantaged groups. The judges play a notably pro-active role, even exercising an 'epistolary' jurisdiction in respect of issues raised by letter and acting on their own motion. Hence the need for the Attorney General's role in vetting applications.

judiciary as one of separation of *functions* rather than of *powers*, there being a common interest in co-operating to eliminate, for example, difficulties in the application of statutes, a process in which the practising legal profession should be actively involved.

PLENARY 3
PARLIAMENT AND THE JUDICIARY II

The theme of parliament and the judiciary was continued in the third plenary session, chaired by Ms Kathleen Keating (Canada, CLA) and addressed by Professor Anton Cooray (Sri Lanka, CLEA), The Hon Mr Justice KM Nagabhushan Rao (India, CMJA), The Hon Mr Justice John Dowd, AO (Australia, CMJA) and The Hon Chief Justice Derek Schofield (Gibraltar, CMJA).

Professor Cooray raised a number of complex questions relating to rules of interpretation of constitutional provisions protecting fundamental rights, particularly those affecting the relationship between judges and parliamentarians.[25] Under the now much criticised but still staunchly defended system of parliamentary supremacy, judges are precluded from questioning the validity of legislation. As the Lord Chancellor reaffirmed in his opening address, it was vital that the courts should not become involved in a process of policy evaluation. Where the courts did have the constitutional power of review over legislation, judges were inevitably called upon to make value judgments, particularly where rights were in conflict. In giving a generous and purposive interpretation to Bills of Rights clauses so as to ensure the full measure of protection for individual rights, judges should avoid usurping the function of the legislature. Inevitably, judges would be criticised for lack of or for excessive boldness. This issue raised questions regarding the qualification and training of judges to perform this delicate balancing exercise.

Judge Rao tackled another highly sensitive issue, the boundaries between the jurisdiction of the legislature and the courts in dealing with corrupt practices involving members of parliament. Should such matters be dealt with by parliament as a matter of privilege or should the courts have a role? Judge Rao's paper examines in some detail the recent seminal Indian case of *PV Narasimha Rao v State*[26] in which the constitutional bench of the Supreme Court considered bribery charges against a sitting prime minister. By a 3-2

---

25 'Bills of Rights and Constitutional Interpretation', below, p 59.
26 1998 (4) SC Cases 626 (the *JMM Bribery* case). See 'Parliamentary Privilege versus The Courts', below, p 65. For an analysis preferring the majority view, see Siddharth Bhatnagar, 'Bribery and immunity in Parliament – an Indian perspective' (1998) 12 Commonwealth Judicial Journal No 4, pp 31–33.

majority, the Supreme Court found that a member of parliament was a 'public servant' for the purposes of prevention of corruption legislation. However, the court upheld the immunity of members of parliament from criminal prosecution in respect of the offer and acceptance of a bribe for the purpose of speaking or giving his or her vote in parliament. In the view of Judge Rao, the Supreme Court missed the opportunity to resolve the question of criminal liability involving bribery of members of parliament.

Judge Dowd discussed various ways of promoting judicial and parliamentary ethics. The Australian Judicial Commission had a disciplinary section, but there was a need to create a culture amongst judges of seeking advice on ethical issues. In New South Wales, there existed an independent commission against corruption and a requirement of disclosure of interests on a public register. Clearer guidelines were needed particularly on subtler forms of corruption. Parliamentary ethics advisers required statutory protection in respect of matters disclosed to them.

Chief Justice Schofield spoke of the particular problems of the judiciary in small jurisdictions such as the Cayman Islands and Gibraltar.[27] Where an appointee was drawn from a small local community, there was inevitably a problem of perception of bias in the light of former known allegiances. However, the appointment of judges from overseas on contract also posed problems, particularly in relation to judicial independence, which were not confined to small jurisdictions:

> A fixed term contract and security of tenure for judges do not reconcile, because a judge does not know whether unpopular decisions are going to rebound upon him or her when the time comes for renewal of contract.[28]

The solution might lie in stronger contractual or statutory protection for judges seeking renewal of their terms. Renewal should be automatic, unless misconduct or incapacity was shown or perhaps where a suitable local candidate was available to replace an overseas judge.[29] Other problems which particularly affected judges in small jurisdictions included those of isolation: judges and their families having to maintain a social reserve which led to a very lonely existence.

In discussion, there was support for disclosure of assets as a means of avoiding corruption. It was also noted that regional co-operation could assist the problem of assignment of judges in small jurisdictions. In the Eastern Caribbean, for example, it was possible to avoid the assignment of a person local to a particular small island to serve there as a judge.[30]

---

27 'Maintaining Judicial Independence in a Small Jurisdiction', below, p 73.
28 Below, p 75.
29 Below, p 76 and see Guidelines, II, 1, below, p 20.
30 See Guidelines, V, 1, p 23.

PLENARY 4
ROLE OF NON-JUDICIAL AND NON-PARLIAMENTARY INSTITUTIONS

The fourth plenary session, chaired by Sir Philip Bailhache (Jersey, CPA), was addressed by Dato' Cyrus Das (Malaysia, CLA), John Hatchard (United Kingdom, CLEA) and Mr Wasim Sajjad (Pakistan, CPA).

Cyrus Das discussed the role of the practising legal profession in promoting the rule of law. He emphasised the inter-relationship between the practising profession and the judiciary.[31] An independent judiciary could not exist without an independent bar. The legal profession had a complex role in society and responsibility to identify the shortcomings in legislation or in government action from the standpoint of civil rights:

> The stand it takes may not be popular and may well be misunderstood. But it does not behove a Bar Council to take a popular stance as opposed to a stand that is in accordance with justice ... It falls upon the Bar Association to advise and comment on legislation touching the legal, personal and property rights of citizens and their liberties ... This function cannot be discharged meaningfully unless the Bar is independent and is free to comment without fear of reprisal or penalty.[32]

An independent legal profession was also vital to economic progress and development:

> Unless investors are confident that they may resort to an independent and non-aligned Bar for advice and representation in their dispute with any party, no matter how powerful or well connected they may be, investors' confidence is likely to deteriorate.[33]

John Hatchard's presentation examined the role of national independent institutions (offices of the ombudsman and human rights commissions) in strengthening the democratic framework in Commonwealth jurisdictions.[34] A key element in this process was the development of an effective partnership between parliament and the national institutions. Parliament had a crucial responsibility in ensuring the independence and effectiveness of these bodies in relation to appointments, funding and other resources. The national institutions in their turn should have formal responsibility to parliament and could, and perhaps should, play a major role in advising and providing information for parliamentarians in crucial areas where parliamentarians, particularly in developing countries, appear to operate in an 'information

---

31 'The Practising Legal Profession', below, p 81.

32 Below, p 85. See Guidelines,VIII, 3, p 27.

33 Below, p 86.

34 'Parliamentarians, National Institutions and the Implementation of the Harare Commonwealth Declaration', below, p 89.

vacuum'. He drew attention to an example from Zimbabwe where it appeared that an important constitutional amendment affecting human rights had been rushed through parliament without adequate explanation to members:

> This example emphasises the danger of legislation being passed in circumstances where parliamentarians are seemingly not fully informed of its implications. It follows that MPs must have access to objective and independent information and advice.[35]

Human rights commissions were ideally suited to providing information regarding compliance by the state with international human rights obligations and notice of local human rights violations. The 'partnership' approach of the New Zealand Human Rights Commission provided an excellent model for the development of the relationship between parliamentarians and national institutions.[36] The proposed Guidelines should reflect these concerns.[37]

Mr Sajjad examined a number of mechanisms for ensuring the accountability of government to parliament. The major constitutional instrument of a confidence motion needed to be protected by legislation against floor-crossing, so that a member who changed party lost his/her seat. Parliamentary scrutiny of the executive required that ministers should be answerable for their conduct to parliament on a day to day basis through questions on the floor of the house and through appearance before parliamentary committees. Outside parliament, a free and independent press had a vital role as had the electronic media.

In discussion, there was some lively dissent from Mr Sajjad's support for anti floor-crossing legislation. While it was arguable that a member who left the party under whose ticket he/she was elected should seek a fresh mandate from the electorate, such legislation might be regarded as undemocratic, particularly where, as in Pakistan, it applied where a member was expelled from the party.[38]

There was emphasis on the need for solidarity amongst associations of legal professionals in the face of threats to the rule of law and the importance of the Commonwealth legal non-governmental organisations in this regard. Various ways of strengthening the role of parliament were discussed, including the provision of research capacity to provide access to non-partisan information. The role of an independent Auditor reporting to parliament was recognised as was the need to ensure that standing committees, particularly the public accounts committee, were not dominated by government.[39]

---

35 Below, p 99.
36 Below p 101.
37 See Guidelines, VIII, 7, below, p 27.
38 See Guidelines, III, 2, below, p 21.
39 See Guidelines, VI, 2(a), below, p 24.

PLENARY 5
RELATIONSHIPS WITH THE EXECUTIVE

The fifth plenary session, chaired by the Hon Mr Justice John Dowd (Australia, CMJA), was addressed by Dr Rodger Chongwe, SC (Zambia, CLA) and Professor Robert Martin (Canada, CLEA).

Dr Chongwe considered administrative law controls through judicial review of executive action.[40] He noted that in Africa, the development of judicial review has been linked to detention cases, although much depended upon the willingness of judges to go behind the detention order to ascertain the reasons for the order. There was a need for international assistance in developing administrative law in many Commonwealth jurisdictions. In this connection, the seminars organised by the Legal and Constitutional Affairs Division of the Commonwealth Secretariat had been of great value to judges, civil servants, police and practitioners alike.[41]

Professor Martin spoke about freedom of expression, on which all the objectives of the Colloquium were dependent. He drew attention to the Statement on Freedom of Expression for the Commonwealth, particularly paragraph 2 requiring express constitutional guarantees of freedom of expression and paragraph 4 dealing with state security and public order. The latter paragraph deplored the use of colonial emergency provisions (which should be repealed) and the use of the law of criminal libel to control expression.[42]

In discussion, it was emphasised that decision-makers should be obliged to give substantive reasons for their decisions: legislation should avoid ouster clauses and the conferring of over-wide discretion on the executive. It was noted that the South African Constitution embodied a right to administrative justice implemented by an Open Democracy Act.[43]

---

40 'Judicial Review of Executive Action: Government under the Law', below, p 103.

41 Below, p 108. See, also, Guidelines, VI, 2(b), below, p 25.

42 The Statement on Freedom of Expression for the Commonwealth is set out in Appendix 2, below, p 141.

43 See section 33 of the Constitution of the Republic of South Africa, 1996.

PLENARY 6
JUDGES, PARLIAMENTARIANS AND CIVIL SOCIETY

The sixth plenary session, chaired by Dr Peter Slinn (United Kingdom, CLEA), was addressed by Mr Colin Nicholls, QC (CLA, UK), The Rt Hon Paul East, QC, MP (New Zealand, CPA) and The Hon Justice Rasheed Razvi (Pakistan, CMJA).

Colin Nicholls, in considering the public perception of judges and parliamentarians, noted that, whereas, according to opinion polls conducted in England, there had been a slight decline, to 68%, in the proportion of people who trusted judges to tell the truth, in the case of government ministers and politicians, the figures had declined to 11% and 14% respectively.[44] Mr Nicholls noted that the government response to public anxiety about 'sleaze' in the United Kingdom had been to set up a 'Committee on Standards in Public Life' chaired by a Law Lord, Lord Nolan. While the Nolan Report disclosed some confusion as to what was acceptable behaviour in society generally and particularly within government, the global picture was grimmer. So far as the world in general was concerned, there was a culture of corruption endowed by custom with an acceptability no longer to be tolerated. Codes of conduct required provision for educating civil society, that is, the people, as to how those codes would be observed by judges and parliamentarians. Only in that way could the people have a true perception of the integrity of government.[45]

Paul East addressed the colloquium on the theme of parliamentary privilege and the sub judice rule.[46] He began by pointing out that press freedom was dependent on access to information. Statutory guarantees of freedom of information such as the New Zealand Official Information Act 1982 were therefore of great value. Whether express statutory guarantees of press freedom were necessary depended on local circumstances. The New Zealand experience was that relations between parliament and the judiciary were governed by a doctrine of mutual restraint. Thus the law requires that the courts do not question the proceedings of parliament. On the other hand, parliament will not discuss pending court cases if there is a danger of prejudice to the case in question. The most important parliamentary privilege, freedom of speech, was protected by Article 9 of the Bill of Rights, 1688. Although this did not preclude the reporting of parliamentary proceedings or the giving of factual evidence in court of what occurred in parliament, there

---

44 'Judges and Parliamentarians: The Public Perception', below, p 111.
45 Below, p 114.
46 'Free Speech: Parliamentary Privilege and the Sub Judice Rule', below, p 117.

must be no abridgement of the protection of members from court action for anything they might say in parliament.[47]

Justice Razvi drew on the experience of Pakistan in analysing the relationship between judges and parliamentarians.[48] Historically, they were drawn from different sections of Pakistani society. Many MPs represented the land-owning classes, whereas the judges tended to be drawn from the ranks of the urban middle class intelligentsia. Parliamentary leaders were unresponsive to public opinion and their autocratic tendencies had given rise to judicial activism. This tendency towards autocracy had at times found expression in outright military rule. The judges had been left as upholders of the rule of law: in the face of governmental and parliamentary hostility:

> The public perception in Pakistan with reference to the judiciary is that the common person expects from the judges that they will rise to the occasion in order to protect and uphold their fundamental rights and protect them from repressive laws enacted by parliament.[49]

In discussion, there was general support for the need to strengthen civil society so as to create a culture inimical to intimidation of judges and of parliamentarians and to curtailment of press freedom. The proposed Guidelines should promote co-operation between government and civil society and draw strength from co-operation between the sponsoring organisations and other elements in the community.

PLENARIES 7 AND 8
ADOPTION OF DRAFT GUIDELINES

The final plenaries (chaired by Mr Arthur Donahoe, QC (Secretary General, CPA) and Dr Peter Slinn (Vice President, CLEA)) were devoted to the adoption by consensus of the draft Guidelines prepared as a result of the deliberations in three workshops and an ad hoc drafting committee consisting of representatives of the four sponsoring organisations.

Issues which emerged from the deliberations of the individual workshops (see Appendix 1) included:

- **Dialogue between judiciary and government**. The final wording of the Guidelines reflects the concerns of those who felt that any positive encouragement of dialogue between the government and the judiciary on policy matters might compromise judicial independence.[50]

---

47 Guidelines, III, 1, below, p 21.
48 'Judges and Parliamentarians: The Public Perception', below, p 123.
49 Below, p 127.
50 Guidelines, I, 5, below, p 19. Cf Appendix 1, below, p 132.

- **Judicial appointments**. The words 'in jurisdictions that do not have an appropriate independent process in place' were inserted in order to meet the concerns of those jurisdictions having satisfactory existing procedures which do not involve a formally constituted commission.[51]

- **Security of parliamentarians**. The issue of expulsion of members as a penalty for leaving the party for which he/she was elected provoked perhaps the most serious difference of view. There was strong feeling that any legislation against floor-crossing was a severe threat to the independence of members. However, the experience of some jurisdictions suggested that such legislation was an essential weapon against corruption of members. The eventual wording acknowledged the potential threat to independence of such measures but accepted their necessity in the context of corruption.[52]

---

51 Guidelines, II, 1, below, p 20. See, also, Appendix 1, below, p 134.
52 Guidelines, III, 2(a), below, p 21. Cf proposals regarding accountability of individual members of Parliament, Appendix 1, below, p 134.

CHAPTER 2

LATIMER HOUSE GUIDELINES FOR THE COMMONWEALTH

19 June 1998

Guidelines on good practice governing relations between the executive, parliament and the judiciary in the promotion of good governance, the rule of law and human rights to ensure the effective implementation of the Harare Principles.

PREAMBLE

RECALLING the renewed commitment at the 1997 Commonwealth Heads of Government Meeting at Edinburgh to the Harare Principles and the Millbrook Commonwealth Action Programme and, in particular, the pledge in paragraph 9 of the Harare Declaration to work for the protection and promotion of the fundamental political values of the Commonwealth:

- democracy;
- democratic processes and institutions which reflect national circumstances, the rule of law and the independence of the judiciary;
- just and honest government;
- fundamental human rights, including equal rights and opportunities for all citizens regardless of race, colour, creed or political belief;
- equality for women, so that they may exercise their full and equal rights.

Representatives of the Commonwealth Parliamentary Association, the Commonwealth Magistrates' and Judges' Association, the Commonwealth Lawyers' Association and the Commonwealth Legal Education Association meeting at Latimer House in the United Kingdom from 15 to 19 June 1998:

HAVE RESOLVED to adopt the following **Principles and Guidelines** and propose them for consideration by the Commonwealth Heads of Government Meeting and for effective implementation by member countries of the Commonwealth.

PRINCIPLES

The successful implementation of these Guidelines calls for a commitment, made in the utmost good faith, of the relevant national institutions, in particular, the executive, parliament and the judiciary, to the essential principles of good governance, fundamental human rights and the rule of law, including the independence of the judiciary, so that the legitimate aspirations of all the peoples of the Commonwealth should be met.

Each institution must exercise responsibility and restraint in the exercise of power within its own constitutional sphere so as not to encroach on the legitimate discharge of constitutional functions by the other institutions.

It is recognised that the special circumstances of small and/or under-resourced jurisdictions may require adaptation of these Guidelines.

It is recognised that redress of gender imbalance is essential to accomplish full and equal rights in society and to achieve true human rights. Merit and the capacity to perform public office regardless of disability should be the criteria of eligibility for appointment or election.

GUIDELINES

I   Parliament and the judiciary

1   The legislative function is the primary responsibility of parliament as the elected body representing the people. Judges may be constructive and purposive in the interpretation of legislation, but must not usurp parliament's legislative function. Courts should have the power to declare legislation to be unconstitutional and of no legal effect. However, there may be circumstances where the appropriate remedy would be for the court to declare the incompatibility of a statute with the Constitution, leaving it to the legislature to take remedial legislative measures.

2   Commonwealth parliaments should take speedy and effective steps to implement their countries' international human rights obligations by enacting appropriate human rights legislation. Special legislation (such as equal opportunity laws) is required to extend the protection of fundamental rights to the private sphere. Where domestic incorporation has not occurred, international instruments should be applied to aid interpretation.

3   Judges should adopt a generous and purposive approach in interpreting a Bill of Rights. This is particularly important in countries which are in the process of building democratic traditions. Judges have a vital part to play in developing and maintaining a vibrant human rights environment throughout the Commonwealth.

4   International law and, in particular, human rights jurisprudence can greatly assist domestic courts in interpreting a Bill of Rights. It also can help expand the scope of a Bill of Rights making it more meaningful and effective.

5   While dialogue between the judiciary and the government may be desirable or appropriate, in no circumstances should such dialogue compromise judicial independence.

6   People should have easy and unhindered access to courts, particularly to enforce their fundamental rights. Any existing procedural obstacles to access to justice should be removed.

7   People should also be made aware of, and have access to, other important fora for human rights dispute resolution, particularly Human Rights Commissions, Offices of the Ombudsman and mechanisms for alternative dispute resolution.

8   Everyone, especially judges, parliamentarians and lawyers, should have access to human rights education.

II Preserving judicial independence

1 Judicial autonomy

In jurisdictions that do not already have an appropriate independent process in place, judicial appointments should be made on merit by a judicial services commission or by an appropriate officer of state acting on the advice of such a commission.

Judicial appointments should normally be permanent; whilst in some jurisdictions, contract appointments may be inevitable, such appointments should be subject to appropriate security of tenure.

The judicial services commission should be established by the Constitution or by statute, with a majority of members drawn from the senior judiciary.

Appointments to all levels of the judiciary should have, as an objective, the achievement of equality between women and men.

Judicial vacancies should be advertised. Recommendations for appointment should come from the commission.

2 Funding

Sufficient funding to enable the judiciary to perform its functions to the highest standards should be provided.

Appropriate salaries, supporting staff, resources and equipment are essential to the proper functioning of the judiciary.

As a matter of principle, judicial salaries and benefits should be set by an independent commission and should be maintained.

The administration of monies allocated to the judiciary should be under the control of the judiciary.

3 Training

A culture of judicial education should be developed.

Training should be organised, systematic and ongoing and under the control of an adequately funded judicial body.

Judicial training should include the teaching of the law, judicial skills and the social context, including ethnic and gender issues.

The curriculum should be controlled by judicial officers who should have the assistance of lay specialists.

For jurisdictions without adequate training facilities, access to facilities in other jurisdictions should be provided.

Courses in judicial education should be offered to practising lawyers as part of their ongoing professional development training.

III   Preserving the independence of parliamentarians

1   Article 9 of the Bill of Rights 1688 is re-affirmed. This article provides:

That the Freedome of Speech and Debates or Proceedings in Parlyement ought not to be impeached or questioned in any court or place out of Parlyement.

2   Security of members during their parliamentary term is fundamental to parliamentary independence and therefore:

(a) the expulsion of members from parliament as a penalty for leaving their parties (floor-crossing) should be viewed as a possible infringement of members independence; anti-defection measures may be necessary in some jurisdictions to deal with corrupt practices;

(b) laws allowing for the recall of members during their elected term should be viewed with caution, as a potential threat to the independence of members;

(c) the cessation of membership of a political party of itself should not lead to the loss of a member's seat.

3   In the discharge of their functions, members should be free from improper pressures and accordingly:

(a) the criminal law and the use of defamation proceedings are not appropriate mechanisms for restricting legitimate criticism of the government or the parliament;

(b) the defence of qualified privilege with respect to reports of parliamentary proceedings should be drawn as broadly as possible to permit full public reporting and discussion of public affairs;

(c) the offence of contempt of parliament should be drawn as narrowly as possible.

IV   Women in parliament

1   To improve the numbers of women members in Commonwealth parliaments, the role of women within political parties should be enhanced, including the appointment of more women to executive roles within political parties.

2   Pro-active searches for potential candidates should be undertaken by political parties.

3   Political parties in nations with proportional representation should be required to ensure an adequate gender balance on their respective lists of candidates for election. Women, where relevant, should be included in the top part of the candidates lists of political parties. Parties should be called upon publicly to declare the degree of representation of women on their lists and to defend any failure to maintain adequate representation.

4   Where there is no proportional representation, candidate search and/or selection committees of political parties should be gender balanced as should representation at political conventions and this should be facilitated by political parties by way of amendment to party constitutions; women should be put forward for safe seats.

5   Women should be elected to parliament through regular electoral processes. The provision of reservations for women in national constitutions, whilst useful, tends to be insufficient for securing adequate and long term representation by women.

6   Men should work in partnership with women to redress constraints on women entering parliament. True gender balance requires the oppositional element of the inclusion of men in the process of dialogue and remedial action to address the necessary inclusion of both genders in all aspects of public life.

V Judicial and parliamentary ethics

1 Judicial ethics

(a) A Code of Ethics and Conduct should be developed and adopted by each judiciary as a means of ensuring the accountability of judges;

(b) the Commonwealth Magistrates' and Judges' Association should be encouraged to complete its Model Code of Judicial Conduct now in development;

(c) the Association should also serve as a repository of codes of judicial conduct developed by Commonwealth judiciaries, which will serve as a resource for other jurisdictions.

2 Parliamentary ethics

(a) Conflict of interest guidelines and Codes of Conduct should require full disclosure by ministers and members of their financial and business interests;

(b) members of parliament should have privileged access to advice from statutorily established Ethics Advisors;

(c) whilst responsive to the needs of society and recognising minority views in society, members of parliament should avoid excessive influence of lobbyists and special interest groups.

VI   Accountability mechanisms

1   Judicial accountability

(a) Discipline:

    (i) in cases where a judge is at risk of removal, the judge must have the right to be fully informed of the charges, to be represented at a hearing, to make a full defence, and to be judged by an independent and impartial tribunal. Grounds for removal of a judge should be limited to:

    (A) inability to perform judicial duties; and

    (B) serious misconduct;

    (ii) in all other matters, the process should be conducted by the chief judge of the courts;

    (iii) disciplinary procedures should not include the public admonition of judges. Any admonitions should be delivered in private, by the chief judge.

(b) Public criticism:

    (i) legitimate public criticism of judicial performance is a means of ensuring accountability;

    (ii) the criminal law and contempt proceedings are not appropriate mechanisms for restricting legitimate criticism of the courts.

2   Executive accountability

(a) Accountability of the executive to parliament:

Parliamentary procedures should provide adequate mechanisms to enforce the accountability of the executive to parliament. These should include:

    (i) a committee structure appropriate to the size of parliament, adequately resourced and with the power to summon witnesses, including ministers. Governments should be required to announce publicly, within a defined time period, their responses to committee reports;

    (ii) standing orders should provide appropriate opportunities for members to question ministers and full debate on legislative proposals;

    (iii) the Public Accounts should be independently audited by the Auditor General who is responsible to and must report directly to parliament;

(iv) the chair of the Public Accounts Committee should normally be an opposition member;

(v) offices of the Ombudsman, Human Rights Commissions and Access to Information Commissioners should report regularly to parliament.

(b) Judicial review

Commonwealth governments should endorse and implement the principles of judicial review enshrined in the Lusaka Statement on Government under the Law.

VII The law-making process

1 Women should be involved in the work of national law commissions in the law-making process. Ongoing assessment of legislation is essential so as to create a more gender balanced society. Gender-neutral language should be used in the drafting and use of legislation.

2 Procedures for the preliminary examination of issues in proposed legislation should be adopted and published so that:

(a) there is public exposure of issues, papers and consultation on major reforms including, where possible, a draft bill;

(b) standing orders provide a delay of some days between introduction and debate to enable public comment unless suspended by consent or a significantly high percentage vote of the chamber; and

(c) major legislation can be referred to a select committee allowing for the detailed examination of such legislation and the taking of evidence from members of the public.

3 Model standing orders protecting members' rights and privileges and permitting the incorporation of variations, to take local circumstances into account, should be drafted and published.

4 Parliament should be serviced by a professional staff independent of the regular public service.

5 Adequate resources to government and non-government back benchers should be provided to improve parliamentary input and should include provision for:

(a) training of new members;

(b) secretarial, office, library and research facilities;

(c) drafting assistance including private members bills.

6 An all-party committee of members of parliament should review and administer parliament's budget which should not be subject to amendment by the executive.

7 Appropriate legislation should incorporate international human rights instruments to assist in interpretation and to ensure that ministers certify compliance with such instruments, on introduction of the legislation.

8 It is recommended that 'sunset' legislation (for the expiry of all subordinate legislation not renewed) should be enacted subject to power to extend the life of such legislation.

VIII The role of non-judicial and non-parliamentary institutions

1   The Commonwealth Statement on Freedom of Expression (set out in Appendix 2) provides essential guarantees to which all Commonwealth countries should subscribe.

2   The executive must refrain from all measures directed at inhibiting the freedom of the press, including indirect methods such as the misuse of official advertising.

3   An independent, organised legal profession is an essential component in the protection of the rule of law.

4   Adequate legal aid schemes should be provided for poor and disadvantaged litigants, including public interest advocates.

5   Legal professional organisations should assist in the provision, through pro bono schemes, of access to justice for the impecunious.

6   The executive must refrain from obstructing the functioning of an independent legal profession by such means as withholding licensing of professional bodies.

7   Human Rights Commissions, Offices of the Ombudsman and Access to Information Commissioners can play a key role in enhancing public awareness of good governance and rule of law issues and adequate funding and resources should be made available to enable them to discharge these functions. Parliament should accept responsibility in this regard.

Such institutions should be empowered to provide access to alternative dispute resolution mechanisms.

IX   Measures for implementation and monitoring compliance

These guidelines should be forwarded to the Commonwealth Secretariat for consideration by Law Ministers and Heads of Government.

If these Guidelines are adopted, an effective monitoring procedure, which might include a Standing Committee, should be devised under which all Commonwealth jurisdictions accept an obligation to report on their compliance with these Guidelines.

Consideration of these reports should form a regular part of the Meetings of Law Ministers and of Heads of Government.

CHAPTER 3

PARLIAMENTARY SOVEREIGNTY AND JUDICIAL INDEPENDENCE: KEYNOTE ADDRESS

Lord Irvine of Lairg

I was delighted to be asked to give the opening address at this Joint Colloquium. It always gives me great pleasure to meet colleagues from around the Commonwealth; and to participate in events which make the bonds between our countries grow ever stronger.

The purpose of this Colloquium is to devise a strategy to strengthen the democratic framework within Commonwealth jurisdictions, in harmony with the Harare Declaration – a pledge made by Heads of Government, in 1991, to work with renewed vigour to protect and promote the values of democracy; just and honest government; the rule of law; and the independence of the judiciary throughout the Commonwealth. You have set yourselves an ambitious task. I applaud it. By the end of this Colloquium, you will have considered many of the key issues facing all nations committed to democracy and the rule of law – the fundamental building blocks for a modern, decent society.

The sovereignty of parliament; maintaining the separation of powers and the independence of the judiciary; upholding human rights; and the proper role of political parties. All these issues are on your agenda. With such a well qualified group of participants, representing such a wide range of experience and practice, your discussion over the next three days will be both enlightening and purposeful. In the time allotted to me, I can only touch on a few of these issues. My aim is to highlight their enormous importance rather than to influence or second-guess your discussion. I will be interested to hear your views, and to learn more about you conclusions, in due course.

Let us begin with first principles. Before we can discuss how to strengthen democracy or judicial independence, we must first establish the relationship between the various arms of government. The British Constitution, largely unwritten, is based firmly on the separation of powers. Parliament makes the laws; the judiciary interprets them; and the judiciary develops the common law. Parliament also confers all manner of powers on the executive and other bodies. It is for the courts to ensure that those powers are neither exceeded nor abused, but exercised lawfully.

Judicial review – a subject I know you will be discussing during the next few days – promotes the rule of law. There should be no political – and most certainly no party political – aspect to judicial review. In exercising their powers of judicial review, the judges should never give grounds for the public to believe that they intend to reverse government policies simply because they dislike them. The court does not substitute its opinion for that of the decision-maker on whom parliament has conferred the power of decision. The court rules only on the legality of a decision – not its correctness. In doing so, the court is not acting against the will of parliament, but in support of it. That is how it should be.

The separation of powers represents a delicate balance. Its success depends on continued public confidence in the political impartiality of our judges. I am sure there is no question mark over the political impartiality of Britain's judges in the 1990s. And it is precisely because of that public confidence that judges are entrusted by government with inquiries into areas of the highest political sensitivity.

In some countries, including Australia, involvement by judges in government commissions or inquiries is thought inconsistent with judicial independence from the executive. That has not been our position. I could give you many examples of judicial inquiries we think of the highest value. Take Lord Woolf's inquiry into the disturbances at Strangeways Prison and the late Lord Taylor's inquiry into the Hillsborough football stadium disaster. Current examples are Lord Justice Philip's inquiry into the BSE crisis and Lord Saville's inquiry into the events of Bloody Sunday.

Speaking in 1993, Lord Bingham, now the Lord Chief Justice, then the Master of the Rolls, said that it was, in his opinion:

> ... consistent with judicial office for a judge to serve ... [on a committee or inquiry] if the reason for his [or her] appointment is the need to harness to the task in question the special skills which a judge should possess: characteristically, the ability to dissect and analyse evidence; appraise witnesses; exercise a fair and balanced judgment; write a clear and coherent report, and so on.

That can be the only justification for asking a judge to serve in this way. And it is surely the reason why, as soon as a problem needing independent investigation is revealed, that the press, the public, and, very often, politicians take up the call for a judicial inquiry. Chairing by a serving judge invests inquiries not only with dignity. It gives them a vital detachment from the hurly-burly and pressures of political life under a person who, it will be accepted, is impartial because he or she is a judge.

I sometimes think that we do not give sufficient acknowledgement to the enormous additional public service which these judges give to our country. As Lord Woolf said in the House of Lords in 1996:

> ... it is a role which the judiciary do not seek but which is thrust upon them. But they accept the responsibility because they recognise that it is thought ... in the public interest that they do so.

I take this opportunity to express my thanks and appreciation to all those judges who have served, are serving, and will serve in the future as heads of public inquiries.

Involvement in inquiries is one way in which our judges help promote good government and better public administration. They are, of course, comparatively rare. Judicial review is more common. In this country, it has often, and rightly, held the executive to account. It has improved the quality of administrative decision-making. But there is no question of our judges misusing the opportunities presented by judicial review in an attempt to establish themselves as a power to rival the sovereignty of parliament.

The ultimate sovereignty of parliament is central to the British Constitution. You will know of the British government's commitment to constitutional reform. Our reform programme is wide-ranging, encompassing devolution to Scotland and Wales; a new Mayor and elected authority for London; a new Northern Ireland settlement; electoral reform; a Human Rights Bill; freedom of information legislation; and much more. This programme is ambitious and radical. But at its heart remains an unshakeable commitment to upholding parliamentary sovereignty.

Many of these constitutional changes will have implications for our judges and courts. For example, devolution will confer on the British judiciary a wholly new function of a constitutional character since it is the judicial system, in the shape of the Judicial Committee of the Privy Council, which will bear ultimate responsibility for ensuring that the new Scottish parliament does not transgress the bounds of its legislative competence.

However, from the judges' perspective, probably the most significant element in our reform programme is our commitment to giving greater effect to the European Convention on Human Rights in British law. The Human Rights Bill is currently at the Committee Stage in the House of Commons. At the moment our law possesses no statute which systematically sets out our citizens' rights. This sets us apart from a number of our Commonwealth neighbours, including Canada, which adopted a Charter of Rights and Freedoms in 1982, and New Zealand, which passed a Bill of Rights Act in 1990. The United Kingdom is bound to uphold the rights set out in the European Convention on Human Rights but our own courts cannot enforce those rights directly, even in the face of a clear infringement of fundamental rights. They can only take account of them.

Over the years, parliament has given us some legislation which provides protection for aspects of human rights, most notably in the areas of sex and race equality; but, today, British citizens have no comprehensive protection for their rights in their own domestic justice system. Our judges are in a difficult position. They do not want to act contrary to the will of parliament. In the United Kingdom, the executive, legislative and judicial branches of government are not equal and co-ordinate. Parliament is the senior partner. Our judges recognise that. At the same time, they want to play a full part in developing United Kingdom law so that fundamental human rights are better understood and protected.

Within the boundaries of the law and their jurisdiction, our courts have increasingly tried to defend human rights, particularly through the process of judicial review. Though British courts are constrained by the doctrine of parliamentary sovereignty from reviewing primary legislation itself, their supervisory powers have nevertheless contributed substantially to human rights protection in two key ways.

First, by imposing requirements of fairness and rationality on public decision-makers, judicial review ensures that individuals are not subjected to arbitrary treatment by those entrusted with governmental power. Secondly, the courts subject executive action, which impacts on fundamental rights, to particularly thorough scrutiny. This is undoubtedly important. However, judicial review cannot, by itself, secure human rights. That is not its core purpose.

The Human Rights Bill presents a new way forward. It will, for the first time, provide the United Kingdom with a modern charter of fundamental human rights, enforceable in national courts, while, at the same time, upholding the sovereignty of parliament. Let me take a moment to explain how the regime established by the Human Rights Bill will work in practice.

When a Bill is introduced into parliament, the responsible government Minister will have to give an assurance that the proposed legislation is compatible with the terms of the European Convention. If he or she cannot do that, then parliament will have a clear indication that the Bill needs very careful scrutiny. In the next stage, responsibility falls on the judges. The Human Rights Bill requires them to interpret legislation consistently with Convention rights as far as possible. In most cases before them, this means that our judges will be able to give effect to Convention rights. However, in some rare instances, the judges will find legislation to be clearly incompatible. When this happens, the judges will not have the power to disregard or to strike down incompatible Acts. That would place them in conflict with parliament. I believe our judges would not want that. Instead, our higher courts will be able to make a formal declaration that the Act in question is incompatible with the Convention. That puts government on notice that action is required. It sends the problem, and the responsibility for solving it, back where it belongs – to the elected representatives of the people.

It will be for parliament, in partnership with the government, to take the necessary remedial action. The Human Rights Bill encourages corrective action by providing a 'fast-track' procedure for that purpose. This is a significant difference between our approach and the human rights culture in other countries. For example, in the USA, the Constitution is supreme and the courts have the power to strike down laws. In Canada, which has a well developed human rights culture, judges can also strike down legislation which is deemed unconstitutional.

Our approach is closer to that of New Zealand, in which judges cannot disapply legislation which is incompatible with basic human rights. Like New Zealand, we have sought a means of upholding human rights without disturbing the principle of parliamentary sovereignty. Each country must find a solution which is sensitive to its domestic culture. No single template can be made to fit all national circumstances. What works for us will not work for everyone. But we all need to find a way to achieve an effective balance between the powers of the judges and the powers of government and parliament.

Britain's unequivocal commitment to the ultimate sovereignty of parliament will not reduce the efficacy of our new human rights system in practice. The lack of any jurisdiction to strike down incompatible primary legislation will not, in the vast majority of cases, impair the ability of the courts to ensure that the executive and other public authorities exercise their discretionary and rule-making powers consistently with human rights. In addition, although the Human Rights Bill does not disturb the sovereignty of parliament, that sovereignty will, in future, have to be exercised within an environment highly sensitive to fundamental rights. In particular, a declaration by a higher court that British law is incompatible with the European Convention is likely to create immense political pressure to amend the offending legislation to secure the protection of the relevant right in our national law.

Far from being an uneasy compromise, this accommodation between parliamentary sovereignty, the role of the judges and the fundamental importance of human rights lies at the heart of the Bill's strength. By placing principle and modernity side by side, the Bill will ensure a catholic approach leading to the strongest possible foundation for a uniquely British regime of human rights protection. We have found our solution to the conundrum I identified earlier. In doing so, we have learned a great deal from our partners in the Commonwealth. Our experience should contribute yet another building block for comparable developments in other countries.

I have spent a little time exploring the issues raised by judicial review and the Human Rights Bill because they provide excellent illustrations for many of the questions you will be discussing over the next few days. For example – what are the proper boundaries of the relationship between judiciary and parliament? Should courts be able to over-ride the decisions of the elected representatives of the people? How do democracy and the rule of law support each other? To what extent is it possible for these fundamental pillars of a strong, modern society to have differing priorities which bring them into conflict? I have no doubt that you will wrestle with these and many other similar questions over the next few days.

Let me say a few words now about another issue which is high on your agenda: judicial independence. The independence of the judiciary is a cornerstone of Britain's constitutional arrangements. This government will uphold it, for without judicial independence there is no rule of law. It is central to maintaining a fair and just society. I believe that there is no one in this room who would dispute that.

If judges depend on the goodwill of the government for their continuing employment, they may find themselves unable to resist political or other improper interference in individual cases. So, judges must have security of tenure. They must be able to undertake their responsibilities and exercise their discretion without fear or favour. Their appointments and careers must be developed on the basis of objective criteria to avoid any suggestion of favouritism or preferment in return for favours rendered.

I have a great deal of confidence in the judicial appointments process in England and Wales, not least because of the high quality of the judges it produces. But we are far from complacent. Though the judicial appointments process in England and Wales had undergone considerable change in recent years, I entered the office of Lord Chancellor convinced that further reform and modernisation was needed.

Over the past year, many changes have been initiated. The principles of application and open competition for appointment are now at the heart of the judicial appointments process. Transparency has become our watchword. Candidates are assessed against objective criteria. Those criteria are readily available, both in paper form and on the Internet.

It now remains for me to wish you every success in your important deliberations.

THE CONSTITUTION, PARLIAMENT AND THE COURTS: TOWARDS A COMMONWEALTH MODEL

James S Read

The basis for our discussion this week is found in the evolution of parliamentary government, albeit in a variety of forms, in the 54 very diverse Commonwealth countries scattered throughout the world. This version of parliamentary government was derived from the United Kingdom but the development of the export model has involved a number of familiar paradoxes.

1   Throughout the Commonwealth, parliamentary government is established by formal constitutions which provide detailed frameworks for the conduct of government. Yet the United Kingdom itself has never had a written constitution or a supreme law and the actual functioning of its constitutional organs in key areas is determined by so-called 'conventions'. However, the end of this century and millennium sees a number of changes in the United Kingdom which amount to stages in the building of a constitutional edifice: the introduction of new patterns of devolved government for Northern Ireland, Scotland and Wales; and the adoption of the European Convention on Human Rights as part of domestic law, enforceable for the first time in our own courts.

    Although introduced by ordinary legislation, these measures will to a considerable extent enjoy the quality of a written constitution: they will be difficult to amend and almost impossible to repeal within any foreseeable time-scale, and they will significantly change the scope of the judicial function by giving the courts new powers to adjudicate upon the exercise of executive and legislative powers. In fact, we took the first steps towards the adoption of a more formal constitution a quarter of a century ago, when we joined the then European Economic Community, now the European Union; although it was only a few years ago that we discovered that this step had for the first time given our judges the authority, and duty, to examine the validity of Acts of parliament, and to condemn those which did not conform to our European obligations;[1] subject, of course, to the over-riding views of our new Supreme Court, the European Court of Justice.

2   Of course, contrary to many misconceptions, the United Kingdom does not practise the 'separation of powers'. The presence of the Lord

---

1   See *R v Secretary of State for Transport, ex p Factortame Ltd (No 2)* [1989] AC 603.

Chancellor, from the peak of the executive, legislative and judicial branches of our government, is sufficient demonstration of this. The celebrated 'Westminster Model' shared by so many Commonwealth states is predicated upon the close integration of the executive and legislative which survives even in those African and other states which have directly elected executive Presidents (some of whom, indeed, are members of parliament). Separation of powers on the United States model – with ministers appointed from outside parliament – has had only a fragmentary and unsuccessful history in the Commonwealth (for instance, in Nigeria 1979–83).

3   In Commonwealth practice, the 'separation of powers' means in effect the independence of the judiciary. The source of this independence in most states reflects the British experience, the constitutions providing for the qualifications for judges, their mode of appointment and security of tenure and (generous) remuneration. The meaning of this independence is, in essence, that judges and magistrates are free from executive or legislative interference or other improper influences in deciding cases; but it also requires that the courts are accessible to the people (not merely without unnecessary obstacles in their way but with assistance by way of legal aid, etc, where needed); that judges and magistrates alone are free to manage the courts, including allocation of cases; that the judiciary enjoys sufficient resources, within national economic constraints, to deliver timely and effective justice, including an adequate judicial establishment and an effective support service controlled by registrars; that the judicial role is respected by the people and particularly by their rulers; that judgments are obeyed; and that the state does not establish rival tribunals devoid of proper judicial safeguards and procedures. The fruits of judicial independence will then be seen in the quality of justice administered; in upholding the constitution and its values, in protecting human rights and in maintaining the balance between the individual and the state.

4   The 'supremacy' (or even, misleadingly, 'sovereignty') of parliament has long been one of the doctrines offered by British constitutional lawyers, including Dicey. Whatever it may have meant in 19th-century England, the doctrine has been severely dented in the 20th, for example, by our entry into Europe. In any case, it could not survive transplantation into the political order of a new state established by a written constitution which imposed a variety of limitations upon the legislative power: for example, by enforceable guarantees of fundamental rights; or in some cases by federal structures or other forms of devolution of legislative power.

Commonwealth parliaments are established and empowered by constitutions as the seats of constitutional authority, but those constitutions also set limits to their powers. But, under the constitution, parliament is normally given a variety of functions, not merely to enact legislation but also, amongst other things, to control the executive.

5   It is also relevant to acknowledge the significance of the 'freedom of parliament', derived from its diverse role in legislating, controlling the executive, providing a cockpit for the national political debate and redressing individual grievances. This freedom includes especially the individual freedom of speech of members in debate, but it extends to a wider area of parliamentary privilege, granting certain individual and collective immunities and recognising the right of parliament itself to assert certain privileges and to adjudicate upon alleged breaches thereof. (Such matters are usually defined by statute and common law rather than by constitutions).

6   The role of the individual member of parliament is also relevant. Recent developments indicated that the Westminster system itself formerly lacked adequate protection against the abuse of parliamentary rights by individual members. 'Sleaze' alleged in various forms, including alleged 'cash-for-questions', surfaced as a recurrent issue before and at the 1997 General Election (at which one independent member was elected as an 'anti-sleaze' candidate). The Westminster response has been piecemeal: the Register of Members' Interests, special committees and a commissioner. Commonwealth countries have adopted a variety of measures, including Leadership Codes applicable to members of parliament and others.

7   In one respect in particular, recent British experience has greatly enhanced the judicial role in the regulation of government: over the past three decades our judges have revolutionised their approach to the judicial review of government action, reinforced by reform of the procedural rules. After an earlier period of self-denial, the courts now actively engage in the scrutiny of executive action, whether by a government minister (even by a former Lord Chancellor himself, in fixing court fees), a local or other public authority or even an apparently private body exercising some kind of public function. Moreover, by expanding the rules of locus standi, the courts now on occasion act even at the behest of pressure groups and other non-governmental organisations. This has been the greatest judicial development in the United Kingdom in recent years, and one which may not yet be fully appreciated in all Commonwealth jurisdictions.

8   Unlike the traditional British concept of the judicial role, written constitutions inevitably enhance judicial authority by instituting a power of judicial review, because it falls to the judges (usually by express provision) to determine questions which arise as to the exercise of constitutional functions and, in doing so, to interpret the constitutional provisions. This role is normally filled by the High Court and, on final appeal, by the Supreme Court (in South Africa by the unique Constitutional Court).

This function normally includes the power even to 'over rule' parliament by declaring primary legislation (Acts of parliament) to be invalid for breach of constitutional provisions (for example, fundamental rights provisions). In some states, the courts may specify a period within which parliament is required to amend the offending provisions.

On some such matters, judges may recognise that they ultimately exercise a power of subjective 'value-judgment' (as may be required in the application of fundamental rights provisions). British judges, as members of the Judicial Committee of the Privy Council, have on occasion been ready to discern in constitutions key provisions which are not expressly stated therein but which the judges have been willing to 'imply' in order to implement a principle seen as fundamental to the constitution. The High Court of Australia has followed a similar course in inferring freedom of expression as a product of the basic concept of representative government.[2]

---

2   See *Theophanous v Herald and Weekly Times Ltd* [1994] 3 LRC 369, Aust HC.

THE JUDICIARY: QUALIFICATIONS, TRAINING AND GENDER BALANCE

The Hon Justice Dame Silvia Cartwright

The task ahead of me of completing a discourse on the qualifications and training of judicial officers and their gender balance, a subject upon which volumes have been written, speeches made and numerous debates held, is daunting. My attempt to do justice to these subjects brings to mind the words of that well known feminist Samuel Johnson:

> A woman's preaching is like a dog walking on his hind legs. It is not done well, but you are surprised to find it done at all.

The discussion must start from the premise that judicial independence is a principle which exists to enable judges to deliver impartial justice, freed from any improper pressure and influence from any source. As a rule, judges will think first of improper pressure which might be applied from an external source such as parliament, the media or lobby groups. There is, however, another influence which I suggest is a more insidious, potentially harmful and complex obstacle to judicial impartiality. The predisposition to particular world views in every human being is the product of life experiences which influence decision-making. Each judge on appointment, promises to do justice to all people without fear or favour, affection or ill will. The ongoing attempt to do just that in spite of our in-built prejudices, be they conservative or liberal, is an almost insuperable hurdle to delivering even-handed justice. Selecting the right judicial material, striving to have a balance of appropriately qualified judges and training those judges is one way of ensuring that natural prejudices, many of which we judges will believe are positive, are recognised and confronted.

Judicial independence exists for the benefit of the community. As Sir Ninian Stephens, then judge of the High Court of Australia and later Governor General of that country observed: 'What ultimately protects the independence of the judiciary is a community consensus that independence is a quality worth protecting.'

Nor does judicial independence 'imply a privileged position for judges, it is not a licence for idiosyncrasy let alone a passport to step outside the boundaries of the law'.[1] The ability to recognise one's prejudices or

---

1   The Inaugural Neil Williamson Memorial Lecture, 'Judicial Independence Revisited'. Delivered by the Rt Hon Sir Thomas Eichelbaum, Chief Justice of New Zealand, Christchurch, 13 August 1997.

idiosyncrasies and to deliver impartial justice in the interests of the community at large inevitably demands that judicial officers are appointed from the ranks of those whose qualifications are of the highest order. Without the respect of the community, judicial independence will not survive. Incompetent, corrupt, dilatory or even rude judges will seldom now be tolerated. Inevitably there will be pressure from the community or from other branches of government for their control or removal. That the independence of the judiciary is closely tied to the merit of those selected for judicial office is widely recognised. For example, paragraph 10 of the United Nations *Basic Principles on the Independence of the Judiciary*[2] states that persons selected for judicial office:

> ... shall be individuals of integrity and ability with appropriate training or qualifications in law. Any method of judicial selection shall safeguard against judicial appointments for improper motives. In the selection of judges, there shall be no discrimination against a person on the grounds of race, colour, sex, religion, political or other opinion, national or social origin, property, birth or status except that a requirement that a candidate for judicial office must be a national of the country concerned, shall not be considered discriminatory.

QUALIFICATIONS

The first approach in all jurisdictions is that appointments to the judiciary should be made on merit. What then is merit? Academic qualifications and broad experience at the Bar or in academic life are those most routinely cited. But they are not in themselves sufficient. The qualities of the person appointed to the judiciary are at least as important and both are essential. Knowledge of the community which the judge must serve is a fundamental requisite.[3] Of necessity the group from which judges are drawn will be legally educated, the intelligent and the respectable. The vast majority of citizens would not qualify on one or other ground. As the life of the judge will often concern those very citizens, some faint understanding of the factors which influence their lives and actions will undeniably assist decision-making, and as a result help command the respect of the public.

New Zealand judges have recently been asked to specify the different kinds of attributes or experience an effective judge needs. The most frequently mentioned by both men and women judges was wide legal experience, preferably as counsel. Knowledge of the law itself was rated highly by both

---

2   Adopted by the 7th United Nations Congress on the Prevention of Crime and Treatment of Offenders held at Milan, 26 August–6 September 1985 and endorsed by GA Resolution 40/42 of 29 November 1985 and 40/146 of 13 December 1985.

3   As Palmer notes, 'They need social awareness. If they move only in legal circles they will tend to have a narrow range of community knowledge'. See paper entitled 'Judicial Selection and Accountability' by Sir Geoffrey Palmer, former New Zealand Prime Minister and Attorney General.

women and men, followed by experience in the application of the law in specialist areas, an attribute rated more highly by men than by women. Both mentioned 'people skills' as an important aspect of professional experience. But women ranked management skills second, denoting the ability to juggle many different tasks or cope with pressure, after legal experience and ahead of knowledge of the law and people skills.

When asked to list the most important personal qualities an effective judge requires, male judges' most favoured options were fairness, impartiality, intellect, analytical skills, empathy, compassion, courtesy, sensitivity and integrity. Women's favoured options, in order, were empathy, compassion, an ability to listen, fairness, impartiality, common sense, a sense of humour and an even temper. The research demonstrated that there was broad agreement between both men and women judges on the kinds of community experience an effective judge requires. It included wide experience, particularly with other ethnic or socio-economic groups and active participation in a service capacity in the community.[4]

This research was conducted amongst all judges in the New Zealand judicial system, ranging from those in the Court of Appeal to the various divisions of the District Courts and including the Employment and Maori Land Courts. It illustrates what I believe to be a significant advance from the perception that judicial qualifications should be confined to a profound knowledge of the law. Moreover, it recognises that in order to discharge the judicial oath, the qualities of humanity, and knowledge of those in groups other than those from which the judiciary are generally drawn have real significance.

There are, of course, other essential attributes for a modern judge. Drawing on my experience some years ago as Chief Judge of the 100 judges in the District Courts of New Zealand, I would suggest that the ability to cope with stress and long hours of work often on circuit and away from home, and excellent health are factors which should not be overlooked. Personal matters such as financial security and absence of any warning signals such as over-indulgence in alcohol should also be considered. Flexibility of mind and the potential to develop all aspects of a judicial character are also very important. And one participant at this Colloquium has also emphasised the importance of the quality of courage. There ought too, to be a broad age range in the judiciary to provide for the cross-section of views which will emerge from different generations and to ensure a sound line of succession towards seniority. Above all, judges need an ingrained appreciation of their ethical responsibilities.

---

4 'Gender Equality in the New Zealand System: Judges' Perceptions of Gender Issues.' Report of research undertaken by the Judicial Working Group on Gender Equity, November 1996.

JUDICIAL TRAINING

There can be very few jurisdictions which do not now accept the need for judicial training. The euphemisms of the past whereby judges attended programmes of judicial 'studies' rather than education, would be addressed only by other judges, and genuinely believed that any form of compulsory study would interfere with their independence to determine cases impartially, has given way to an appreciation that that was a recipe for stagnation or for the idiosyncratic decision-making that arises from isolation.

Judges no longer burst onto the judicial stage fully trained and knowledgeable in all aspects of the law and its application. Not only does the law itself change too rapidly to enable the modern judge to keep abreast, but the very breadth of judicial work does not permit, except in a small proportion, a claim of expertise or even a level of comfort. There is now a demand from the newly appointed judge for the sort of integrated and systematic programme of judicial studies that can be had from the Bar Associations or Law Societies while still in the profession. Programmes can usefully be developed for study of the law, including both refresher courses and new developments in legislation or the common law.

JUDICIAL SKILLS

Increasingly, there is a need seen for the teaching of judicial skills and for social context education. Judicial skills, such as the ability to write or deliver an oral judgment, or to control a court, to be heard easily in the courtroom, to manage the courtroom technology or the complex and lengthy trial are not necessarily found in every judge. Like the law, they must be learned and for the sake of the public best not learned on the job.

Orientation programmes for newly appointed judges to all levels of the judiciary are now widespread. In New Zealand, such programmes, at least at District Courts level, include a system whereby the new judge will be assigned a mentor to assist during the first few months of judicial work. In the first few days, the new judge will frequently sit with his or her mentor learning life from the other side of the Bench and observing another judge's approach to judging. Peer review and support programmes are being explored in an attempt to ensure the support of colleagues and to provide an organised setting for systematic discussion and consultation. All of these initiatives are designed to improve the quality of judicial work and to reduce pressure on judges so that they become and remain effective and responsive to the changing legal and social factors which have an impact on their judicial work.

SOCIAL CONTEXT EDUCATION

In Canada, social context education is based on the premise that judges have an important and difficult task in adjudicating the multitude of disputes in Canadian society. To do their job well they must be familiar with a wide range of substantive and procedural law, and there is constant pressure to keep that knowledge current. As well, judges seek to strive for fairness and impartiality when deciding individual cases so as to provide equal justice for all litigants.

Social context education serves an important role in the pursuit of fair, impartial and high quality adjudication. As the term implies, social context education deals with the social setting in which judicial decision-making occurs. Canadian society has been transformed by many forces including changing demography, different perception of the role of women, recognition of aboriginal rights and an evolving concept of equality sensitive to difference and diversity. Spurred by the advent of the Canadian Charter of Rights and Freedoms, Canadians have come to realise that judges make important value choices when they decide cases. Moreover, existing rules of law and legal practices are perceived by some as expressing values that are not responsive to the need and desires of many groups in society.

Social context education will often be directed at issues with which many judges, perhaps the majority, may have little familiarity, and in particular at issues of race and gender. Twelve months ago in New Zealand, the entire judiciary attended a three-day programme on 'Gender Issues and the Judiciary' developed to teach something of the reality of women's lives. For a judge to hear first-hand from the complainant in a rape trial; to understand that the gap between men's and women's wages explains why women and particularly Maori women are disproportionately represented in the poorest sectors of society, assists him or her to apply the law more even-handedly. Judges, be they male or female, tend not themselves to have experienced rape or poverty, to have been assaulted in the home or refused credit. The ability to walk in another's shoes for even a few hours is salutary. It enhances the judges' ability to understand why a beaten woman does not always leave home, how society has unintentionally relegated women to the lowest economic sectors in all societies and why so few women are recognised as leaders at the Bar and therefore qualified for appointment to the judiciary. Such education does not interfere with a judge's ability to judge impartially; it enhances it. Knowledge of other people's lives frees the judge from the constraints of his or her life experiences and conditioning.

To be successful, however, any programme of judicial studies must be ongoing, organised, systematic and professionally delivered by a range of presenters. Time must be allocated for the programmes which will be tailored to the requirements of the judge attending, and be evaluated for effectiveness. Educators and speakers from the community are essential, be they legally qualified or with expertise in different skills and experiences. The gifted amateur is no longer sufficient. That may entrench a gifted but amateur judiciary.

GENDER BALANCE

For most of our history, women, for a variety of reasons, have been confined to the private sphere of activity, while men have discharged the duties of public life. Women's advances in education, the fact that they are frequently obliged to work outside the home for an income because they lack the financial support of a husband or male relative, and increasingly the appreciation that to exclude them from public life is a denial of their human rights and a waste of one half of the human resource, means that in the latter part of this century many women are now legally qualified. They continue, however, to face many obstacles to judicial appointment, but complacency, or what I choose to describe as the 'swamp factor', abounds: as the numbers of legally qualified women increase, so too will their proportion in the judiciary. The reality is that the system by which appointments to the judiciary are made favours the status quo. Women are not sufficiently visible or their lifestyles cannot be accommodated, so the 'safe', traditional appointment continues to predominate.

If my premise is accepted: that the modern judge must have qualifications beyond and above knowledge of the law, and to assist them to acquire that knowledge which is outside their every day legal and personal experience, there must be professionally delivered and systematic education, then having a broad range of judicial personnel will greatly assist the process. Those who have other life experiences can learn from each other. But, as importantly, the judiciary will give the appearance of better reflecting the public which it has sworn to serve. Anecdotal accounts from men who protest that they cannot receive justice from a court with a woman judge, registrar and counsel serve to illustrate how women and minority ethnic groups have felt for generations.

If judges are to discharge their judicial oaths then it is necessary to have a mix of judicial officers from a broad variety of backgrounds and with the full range of the finest qualifications and qualities. This promotes a better understanding of other experiences based on differing educational and social backgrounds, ethnicity and gender. As we must acknowledge that we are the product of our social conditioning, education, family background, gender and ethnicity, we cannot truthfully promise the public to be totally unbiased in our judgments. What we can promise, however, is to do all that we can to recognise these influences which might have a bearing on impartiality, and strive nonetheless to be even-handed in the application of the law.

It is therefore, of great importance that the judiciary have an equal balance between men and women: something that I do not think has been achieved in any jurisdiction in the world (with the possible exception of Romania prior to Ceasceau's downfall). It goes without saying that women start with a better understanding about women's lives because that is our conditioning. It does not mean that women judges are biased in favour of women. We, too, have the obligation to set aside any preference except that which is drawn from the evidence before us objectively assessed. But because gender means assumptions about men and women, their behaviours, their natures, and roles that underpin the family, work and social arrangements, it is essential for one half of the population to have one half of the judiciary understand something of their lives while the other half strive to learn more about them.

Efforts to ensure that the goal of equal representation of men and women in the judiciary, appointed on merit, with all the broader understanding of that concept that modern society now holds is not contrary to principle. Most nations espouse the constitutional principle of equality of the sexes and ensure its application in both legislation and policy. All United Nations human rights instruments deriving from the Universal Declaration of Human Rights due to celebrate its 50th anniversary at the end of 1998 recognise that:

> Everyone is entitled to all the rights and freedoms ... without distinction of any kind such as race, colour, sex, language, religion, political or other opinion, national or social origin, property, birth or other status.

In the Convention on the Elimination of All Forms of Discrimination against Women, a United Nations human rights treaty designed to ensure that women achieve both legal and substantive equality in ratifying States, Article 4(1) provides:

> Adoption by States Parties of temporary special measures aimed at accelerating *de facto* equality between men and women shall not be considered discrimination as defined in the present Convention, but shall in no way entail as a consequence the maintenance of unequal or separate standards; these measures shall be discontinued when the objectives of equality of opportunity and treatment have been achieved.

Moreover, Article 7 requires States Parties to:

> ... take all appropriate measures to eliminate discrimination against women in the political and public life of the country, and, in particular, shall ensure to women, on equal terms with men, the right ... to participate in the formulation of government policy and the implementation thereof and to hold public office and perform all public functions at all levels of government ...

As the vast majority of nations within the United Nations family have ratified the Convention for the Elimination of All Forms of Discrimination Against Women, it is probable that every country represented at this symposium is bound by these principles. Moreover, the Commonwealth, in the series of statements originating ten years ago in Bangalore, India, has itself endorsed the need to observe and encourage the implementation of human rights norms by the judiciary. More recently those statements emphasise the need for the judiciary to promote a knowledge and understanding of issues that particularly affect women.

All jurisdictions should therefore be proactive in identifying qualified women for appointment to the judiciary and ensuring that special efforts are made until equality of numbers is achieved. I do not suggest that women will discharge their judicial responsibilities better than men have done for centuries. Nonetheless, they will discharge them differently. These are differences which are to be found in the community and which the public expects to see reflected in its judiciary. As judicial officers, it is our responsibility to work towards achieving judicial independence by ensuring that we understand not only the law which we must apply, but the conditions under which the people who are the raw material in our courts themselves live.

In 1970, a United States lawyer, civil rights activist and feminist said:

> Every form of bigotry can be found in ample supply in the legal system of our country. It would seem that justice (usually depicted as a woman) is indeed blind to racism, sexism, war and poverty.

We have a responsibility to the public and to the judiciary to ensure that a litigant no longer has reason to speak so bitterly of the administration of justice. Our judicial blindness must demonstrate no preference for any person whether vulnerable or powerful, rich or poor, from the minority or dominant culture, male or female. The rule of law depends on it.

46

THE INDEPENDENCE OF THE JUDICIARY WITH SPECIAL REFERENCE TO PARLIAMENTARY CONTROL OF TENURE, TERMS AND CONDITIONS OF SERVICE AND REMUNERATION OF JUDGES: JUDICIAL AUTONOMY AND BUDGETARY CONTROL AND ADMINISTRATION

The Hon Chief Justice Anthony Gubbay

It is a trite observation that the predominant role of the judiciary is to interpret the laws of the land fairly and to dispense justice impartially, and without fear or favour, between individuals or the individual and the State. In this way, the judiciary makes a meaningful contribution to the maintenance of law and order and, consequently, the maintenance of peace within its jurisdiction.

For the judiciary to play its role effectively, it is imperative that it should enjoy an independent status. Its independence is an essential touchstone in the impartial administration of justice and in the adherence to the rule of law.

But, the independence of the judiciary which we talk about should not be constructed to serve the purely personal and selfish ends of judges. For instance, such independence does not mean that judges should report for work late, or not at all, or adjourn cases needlessly. Indeed, the independence of the judiciary does not mean that judges should have different social values from those that exist in our society. Not at all. Such independence must be balanced with responsible professional conduct, competence and integrity on the part of judges. They must not be receptive to influence, inducements, pressures, threats or interference, direct or indirect.

In a sense, therefore, in the exercise of the functions of office, the judge may be said to be responsible for his or her own independence, and all types of unseemly personal behaviour on the part of members of the judiciary should be avoided, as these could have the effect of subverting judicial independence. Examples of such conduct are collaboration between judges and public authorities; making statements which give the impression of bias; serving in politically sensitive capacities; and, particularly in small jurisdictions such as my own, tardiness in adjudicating on matters which involve the executive.

What is required of a judge is the rendering of an honest unbiased opinion based on the law and the facts. This task is far from simple. It demands wisdom as well as knowledge, conscience as well as insight, a sense of balance and proportion; and if no absolute freedom from bias and prejudice, at least the ability to detect and discount such feelings so that they do not becloud the fairness of the judgment. Clearly, these necessary qualities will be endangered substantially unless judges are protected from political, economic or other influences.

HOW IS SUCH PROTECTION ENSURED?

The method of appointing judges is of paramount importance. Never must the motivation be to appoint someone, however able he or she may be, because of an avowed political affiliation.

In terms of the Constitution of Zimbabwe, the Chief Justice and other judges of the Supreme Court and the High Court are appointed by the President after consultation with the Judicial Service Commission. If any proposed appointment is not in accord with the recommendation made by the Judicial Service Commission, the President is enjoined to cause parliament to be informed of the reasons as soon as is practicable. This has never happened. The Judicial Service Commission has as its members the Chief Justice, the Judge President of the High Court, the Attorney General, the Chairman of the Public Service Commission, and two senior and experienced legal practitioners from the private sector. This composition ensures that judicial office is open to all, irrespective of race, creed or the absence of any overt political support for the ruling party. As a matter of reality, the appointments are usually made from senior and experienced legal practitioners in the private sector. Consequently most take office after they have reached mature life and after varied experience in the affairs of society.

In Zimbabwe, judges are appointed until they reach the mandatory age of retirement, 70 years, and not under a fixed term contract. They can only be removed from office by executive action on the ground of professional misconduct (for example, the acceptance of a bribe), or on account of inability, be it mental or physical, to perform the judicial function. Any such removal involves a fairly elaborate procedure laid down in the Constitution of Zimbabwe. If the Chief Justice advises the President that the removal of a judge from office ought to be investigated, the President is enjoined to appoint a tribunal to enquire into the matter and has no option but to comply. In the case of the Chief Justice, it is the President who makes the decision that the incumbent's removal ought to be investigated by a tribunal. Once the question of removal is referred to a tribunal, the judge is suspended from performing the functions of office until the President, on the recommendation of the tribunal or the Judicial Service Commission, either revokes the suspension, or the judge is removed from office.

The tribunal, which must consist of at least three members, is selected by the President from: (a) persons who have held office as a judge in Zimbabwe, or in a country where the official language is English and where judges have unlimited jurisdiction in civil or criminal matters; (b) legal practitioners of not less than seven years standing nominated by the Law Association.

In practical terms, therefore, judges have complete security of tenure during good behaviour and ability to perform their function. Irrespective of the displeasure with which the executive may view a judgment pronounced by a particular judge, it is powerless to remove him or her.

The system is not, however, entirely foolproof to guarantee security of tenure. The President may effectively suspend the Chief Justice from office by appointing a tribunal even though the grounds for investigating the alleged misconduct may be trivial. It would be an improvement if the members of the tribunal were appointed by the Chief Justice and not by the President: and that if the recommendation was to remove the judge, the final say rested upon a resolution being passed by the majority of members of parliament.

Another factor that has considerable bearing on the independence of the judiciary is financial security – the receipt of adequate remuneration. Without it a judge cannot feel independent of the executive. A judge's work and thinking must not be frustrated by lack of money. Many developing countries fall short of this requirement. While the remuneration of judges cannot be expected to compete with the earnings of a reasonably competent legal practitioner in the private sector, it must not fall so far below as to instil a feeling of dependence. It is important that parliaments are alive to the differentiation in income between the public and private sectors, and are receptive to suggestions for effective improvements. Obviously it is embarrassing to place the judiciary at the mercy of Ministers or departments to plead for increases in salary and allowances. This tends to undermine its dignity.

True, the remuneration of judges in most jurisdictions is charged directly on the Consolidated Revenue Fund. This is a safeguard, however symbolic, against the withholding by parliament of necessary financial provision to pay judges. And, under many constitutions, the salary and allowances of judges are protected against reduction. Nonetheless, of greater advantage would be the appointment of a non-government body to recommend to the executive branch how often and to what extent an increase in the remuneration of judges is warranted: and for parliament then to decide the level to which such recommendation can be implemented in the circumstances of the time.

It must never be overlooked that where judicial pay levels are very low, judges often take on other work, sometimes of a nature demeaning of judicial status. This distracts them from their judicial duties. Certainly, also, low pay makes judges vulnerable to corruption.

The dependence of the judiciary on the executive branch for resources is another factor which impairs its independence. The judiciary has no power of the purse. At best, it has to act within the allocation of funds made to it in the annual budget. More often, the allocation of funds is assessed as part of a departmental budget, control over which is exercised by the Minister responsible. Consequently, the judiciary cannot spend a cent more even if it is necessary for streamlining the machinery of justice and improving its performance.

If the judiciary wants to introduce modern science and technology in the functioning of the court system, to expand its facilities, or appoint more judges with a view to expediting the disposal of cases, it cannot do so unless the necessary funds are made available by the executive. Thus, the executive can twist the arm of the judiciary if it does not behave to its liking. This absence of financial autonomy has an adverse impact on the independence of the judiciary as an institution.

There is a need for budgetary independence: that is, the ability of the judiciary to exercise control over its own funds and apply these funds in accordance with its own priorities for a better administration of justice. Much planning goes into an efficient justice delivery system. The judiciary is best left to direct such planning. It is the best agency to determine the priorities. Without budgetary independence all that the judiciary can do is to make the request for funds while the dispensing authority decides, according to its own priorities, what the judiciary gets: and thus, indirectly, in what direction the judiciary develops its operations and machinery. For instance, let it be supposed that a court needs a set of law reports, a number of modern computers and the refurbishing of Judges' Chambers. It makes a request for funds for all three requirements. Nothing stops the allocating authority from providing funds for only one item of its choosing and at its own pace: or no funding at all.

There are further pressures and obstacles which are not as apparent. One of them is preventing a judge from travelling outside the country to attend conferences or seminars by a professed lack of funding to meet the cost of travel and subsistence. Such attendances serve a very useful purpose of bringing judges in other countries together where they can discuss the problems each of them face and how they can be overcome. The unity of judges in different jurisdictions is most essential for securing the independence of domestic judiciaries.

It cannot be gainsaid that the judiciary must be independent with respect to matters of administration bearing directly on the exercise of its judicial function. This specifically includes the assignment of judges, court sittings and court rolls, case management, the allocation of courtrooms, vacations for judges and the direction of court staff. Clearly, a situation in which budgetary control exercised by the executive impacts negatively upon, and undermines, the judiciary's administrative independence, can never be tolerated. It would destroy the judiciary as an institutionalised organ. It would interfere with the separation of powers recognised as imperative to the maintenance of democracy.

In conclusion, it must be emphasised that it is not enough merely to lay down principles for the independence of the judiciary. These principles have to be implemented. Society must be made aware of their importance and any violation of them exposed. In this way, public opinion can be created in defence of the independence of the judiciary and so ensure by necessary outcry that the maintenance of judicial independence is not eroded by the executive.

CHAPTER 7

PARLIAMENTARY SOVEREIGNTY AND 'JUDGE-MADE' LAW; JUDICIAL REVIEW OF LEGISLATION

The Hon Justice Pierré JJ Olivier

It seems as if mankind is doomed (or privileged, the optimist will say) eternally to struggle with its most central problem: how to develop and shape a system to regulate the administration of the affairs of a country, its people and its natural resources which is based not merely on power, expedience, partisan or material interests, but on a legitimate moral basis. The history of these endeavours, the story of the failures and successes, and of the intellectual, practical and even emotional challenges and responses over the centuries are as fascinating as they are important to mankind and its future. No chapter of this history is illustrative of the weaknesses and strengths of our cultural and evolution than that of the sovereignty of parliament.

I use the expression 'sovereignty of parliament' in its formal, juridical sense as describing the relationship between the legislature and the courts. More particularly, I have in mind the English doctrine of the sovereignty of parliament as meaning, in the words of Dicey,[1] that the legislature 'has the right to make or unmake any law whatever' and no person, body or court outside parliament 'is recognised by the law of England as having a right to override or set aside the legislation of parliament'. The legislative authority of parliament is supreme, and the function of the court, in this system, is merely to give effect to these laws. The courts have no right to test or review the laws made by parliament.

This doctrine, which came into vogue in the 17th and 18th centuries in Great Britain as a response to the system of government by a monarch, still reflects the British system of government. As late as 1974, Lord Morris in *Pickin v British Railway Board*[2] stated the position as follows:

> It is the function of the courts to administer the laws which parliament has enacted. In the processes of parliament, there will be much consideration whether a Bill should or should not in one form or another become an enactment. When an enactment is passed, there is finality unless and until it is amended or replaced by parliament. In the courts, there may be argument as to the correct interpretation of the enactment: *there must be none as to whether it should be on the statute book at all.* [My emphasis.]

---

1   Wade, ECS, *The Law of the Constitution*, 10th edn, 1959, p 40.
2   [1974] AC 765, p 789.

Whether the British doctrine of parliamentary supremacy has served the country well that gave it birth is not for me to say. But, let me remind you of the wise words of Lord Scarman:[3]

> It is the helplessness of the law in face of the legislative sovereignty of parliament which makes it difficult for the legal system to accommodate the concept of fundamental and inviolable human rights. Means therefore have to be found whereby (1) there is incorporated into English law a declaration of such rights, (2) these rights are protected against all encroachments, including the power of the state, even when that power is exerted by a representative legislative institution such as parliament.

The doctrine has been abandoned in many Commonwealth states and replaced by the doctrine of constitutional supremacy of the courts, or, simply put, the power of the courts to test or review parliamentary laws against the constitution.

There is an ever-present and abiding reason why the doctrine of parliamentary sovereignty cannot be sustained even in a democratic, multi-party parliamentary system. It lies in the inherent human trait of self-interest and selfishness which, projected into the institution of parliament, inevitably results in the ruling party favouring the partisan interests of its own supporters through its policies and actions while denying even the reasonable claims of others. Such a system cannot guarantee justice. And, in the words of Barker:[4]

> The supreme sovereign which stands in the background of any politically organised community is justice: justice in the sense of that right order of human relations which gives to the greatest possible number of persons the greatest possible opportunity for the highest possible development of all the capacities of the personality.

That a system of parliamentary sovereignty cannot guarantee justice in the Barker sense, at all times and places, is borne out by the horrible experiences of Nazi Germany and apartheid South Africa. The system carries within itself the potential of its own destruction. The world had to find a better system.

It was America's good fortune to lead the world into the new constitutional paradigm. In a unique, creative, inspired two-year period, they conceived and gave birth to a constitution which solved the problem that was seen as the greatest difficulty: '... you must first enable the government to control the governed: and in the next place oblige it to control itself.' The Founding Fathers achieved this ideal by enacting a democratically elected parliament, whose powers were limited by a justiciable Bill of Rights, enforced by a constitutional system of courts with the power to review all legislative and executive acts in the light of the constitution and the Bill of Rights.

---

3   Scarman (Lord), *English Law: The New Dimension*, 1974, p 15.
4   Barker, E, *Principles of Social and Political Theory*, 1951, p 202.

The American model proved so successful that it has been universally acclaimed and followed. By the latest count (undertaken before the break up of the Soviet Union and Yugoslavia), there were 164 countries in the world. All but six of them have written constitutions, the majority of which incorporate a Bill of Rights and an independent judiciary in some form or another.

American jurists are justifiably proud of their constitutional legacy to the world. In a remarkably frank and erudite essay entitled 'The Parchment Barriers', Cahn,[5] the American legal philosopher, shows that only justiciable, constitutional limitations on parliamentary powers can guarantee that judges can uphold justice and fairness in the face of a sovereign parliament that abuses its powers to enact unreasonable and oppressive laws. His theme is that every democratic nation owes a solemn obligation to its judges to curb parliament's powers and to adopt a written bill of rights beyond the reach of the legislature or executive.

It is trite that the American, Canadian and European models of government (to name a few), limited by a human rights regime and enforced by an independent judiciary, serve the interests of society better than any other system. Such models guarantee the most cherished and valuable of all rights, viz the fundamental rights of people. By protecting the rights of all equally and equitably, they ensure a large measure of peace and tranquillity amongst individuals and groups, including minority and ethnic groups.

The unhappy history of my country, doomed by the scourge of apartheid, is well known. But may I remind my colleagues that apartheid could never have come into being without the system of parliamentary sovereignty reigning in our land. We had no bill of rights, and the judicial review of legislation was specifically prohibited by all constitutions prior to the new post-liberation Interim Constitution of 1993. Apart from the horrible consequences of apartheid on millions of people, especially black, coloured and Indian people, apartheid and the system of sovereignty had a debilitating and humiliating effect on our judiciary.

Despite early judicial pronouncements favouring a liberal approach to repressive legislation and a *pro liberate* interpretation, in the end, South African judges, because of the system of parliamentary and executive sovereignty, had to follow a crude positivistic approach. The real tragedy has been that South African judges have had an excellent understanding of justice and morality. Even the fiercest critics of the South African judiciary concede that, using their Roman-Dutch background enhanced by the English law of equity, judges have given admirable judgments in the other fields such as private law and commercial law. What is more, the intolerable position in which they were put by the unjust legislation of parliament and executive decrees was clearly recognised by these judges. I quote but one example.

---

5   Cahn, LL (ed), *Confronting Injustice*, 1962, p 104 *et seq.*

In a judgment in the Transvaal in 1979 (*S v Adams*),[6] King J stated:

> An Act of parliament creates law but not necessarily equity. As a judge in a court of law, I am obliged to give effect to the provisions of an Act of parliament. Speaking for myself and if I were sitting as a court of equity, I would have come to the assistance of the appellant. Unfortunately, and on an intellectually honest approach, I am compelled to conclude that the appeal must fail. [That is, he had to apply the strict letter of the law.]

This attitude was widely held.[7] Under the apartheid cum parliamentary supremacy system, judicial creativity was confined to common law matters, and judicial independence in the true sense of the word became a myth. It became, in the words of Ellmann,[8] 'only another vanity, to be blown away like gossamer by the winds of power' or as, HLA Hart put it, 'a noble dream'.

All this has been changed by the miracle of the transition in our country. In the 1993 Interim Constitution and again in the 1996 Constitution, which is intended to be our permanent constitution, we have done away with parliamentary sovereignty. The Constitution now includes a modern, extensive Bill of Rights, placed out of easy reach of parliament or the executive, and justiciable and enforceable by all the courts of our country, with the Constitutional Court as last court of appeal on constitutional matters. Judges are appointed by a representative Judicial Services Commission chaired by the Chief Justice. Under our system, courts can declare invalid and set aside legislation, and administrative, ministerial and presidential actions if they transgress the Constitution, including the Bill of Rights. Of course, this power of review cannot be exercised arbitrarily. Courts have to follow a two stage enquiry: first, whether the enactment or act in question violates the Bill of Rights, and, secondly, if it does, whether it can be saved by the limitation clause. This clause (section 36 of the 1996 Constitution) reads as follows:

Limitation of rights

36(1) The rights in the Bill of Rights may be limited only in terms of law of general application to the extent that the limitation is reasonable and justifiable in an open and democratic society based on human dignity, equality and freedom, taking into account all relevant factors including:

(a) the nature of the right;

(b) the importance of the purpose of the limitation;

(c) the nature and extent of the limitation;

(d) the relation between the limitation and its purpose; and

(e) less restrictive means to achieve the purpose.

---

6   1979 (4) SA 793 (T), p 801.

7   Davis, D, 'Positivism and the judicial function' [1985] SALJ 103, p113.

8   Ellmann, S, *In Time of Trouble – Law and Liberty in South Africa's State of Emergency*, 1992, p 1.

(2) Except as provided in sub-section (1) or in any other provision of the Constitution, no law may limit any right entrenched in the Bill of Rights.

The first judgment by a court exercising its review powers was delivered early in 1994 under the provisions of the Interim Constitution, which were in all material respects similar to those of the 1996 Constitution. Since then, a large number of cases have dealt with constitutional matters, and judges have exercised their review powers quite liberally. A number of existing legislative provisions have been set aside as incompatible with the interim or permanent Constitutions such as the death penalty and the reverse onus of proof.

Our courts, especially the Constitutional Court, have delved deeply into the philosophy and practice of constitutionalism and human rights. Their judgments are marked by erudition and sophisticated comparative law. Judges now scan African, American, Canadian, British, German and Indian judgments and writings. Foreign constitutions and international treatises are regularly quoted and their rationale given persuasive force. Where judges formerly were virtually reduced to powerless interpreters of rigid apartheid constitutions, they have now achieved their true functions and status: they have become co-architects, and not mere bricklayers, of a new and proud society.

The socio-political and legal philosophy that we have put into practice in South Africa may well cause despair to those accustomed to a high degree of order, finality and certainty. It may well be conceded that our system, in contrast to the system of parliamentary sovereignty, is also imperfect in that judge-made law, even under a constitution, is essentially uncertain, unpredictable, not necessarily what parliament intended, non-static and never finally and for all-time settled.

But, there are at least two redemptive aspects. The first is that already in my country judge-made law, in the sense of the application of the Bill of Rights, has been accepted by the vast majority of our people as just and equitable, legitimate and as an expression of their own moral values. This stands in stark contrast to the reaction to the apartheid laws. And, in this new order, the legitimacy of the judiciary itself has, to a large extent, been restored. Now, for the first time, in the field of constitutional affairs and human rights, justice is seen to be done. The effect of all this is that after nearly a century of shame, our judges can squarely face the community and the world with a legitimate sense of inner contentment and a clear conscience.

The second is that the judiciary, the legislature and our citizens are now travellers into a future that will be built on a common vision of a better world founded on shared moral values. There is a new spirit of vitality, creativity and excitement in all of us. And, in this connection, I wish to quote the eloquent words of Mahomed I, CJ, delivering the Bram Fischer Memorial Lecture in Cape Town on 3 February 1998:

But, the excitement of this pursuit into the future is immeasurably enhanced by the truths absorbed from the past and the present. For lawyers, these include the insistence, at all times, that the attainment of justice must be the rationale for all law; that law cannot be distanced from justice and morality without losing its claim to legitimacy; that the ethical objectives of the law contain the life blood of a nation; that justice must not only be procedurally fair but substantially fair in its execution; that the law must be seen to be fair in its impact on the life of the humblest citizen in search of protection against injustice; that the law is accessible, intelligible, visible and affordable; and that retreat from these truths imperils the very existence and status of a defensible civilisation, first by corrosively destroying within its source of the energy which sustains it and, secondly, by provoking disdain, disorder and rebellion from those it seeks to discipline.

CHAPTER 8

BILLS OF RIGHTS AND CONSTITUTIONAL INTERPRETATION

MJA Cooray

The rules of interpretation appropriate for a Bill of Rights in a common law jurisdiction have their origin in the common law rules of statutory interpretation. They take their special flavour from rules of constitutional interpretation first developed in the United States of America. Bills of Rights are invariably modelled on international and regional human rights declarations and conventions, and, for that reason, interpretation of such international instruments naturally influences domestic courts. The result of this rich diversity of sources is that courts have a spectrum of choices ranging from solemn deference to legislative intention[1] to adventurous judicial activism reaffirming that the judiciary is after all not the 'least dangerous branch' of government.[2]

STATUTORY INTERPRETATION

A question very often asked is whether common law rules of interpretation are adequate in dealing with a Bill of Rights. The common law proceeds on the premise that civil liberties are fully operative in the absence of prohibition, although it is not uncommon for statutes to grant rights and freedoms to people. The accompanying doctrine of legislative supremacy of parliament enables the legislature to take away or restrict common law rights and ensures that courts do not have the power to question the validity of legislation. As the Lord High Chancellor of Great Britain said last year at a human rights conference: 'It is vital that courts should not become involved in a process of policy evaluation which goes beyond its allotted constitutional role [of interpreting legislation]',[3] a view he reaffirmed yesterday. The Supreme Court of India said in 1986 that judges will naturally be influenced by their beliefs

---

1   'It is right that we should preserve as much of the will of Parliament as possible; and so far as that will, as expressed in a statute, is not repugnant to the Constitution, we should uphold those provisions which we consider not to conflict with the Constitution': *Senadhira v The Bribery Commissioner* (1961) 63 Ceylon New Law Reports 313, p 321, *per* Sansoni CJ (SC).

2   Bickel, A, *The Least Dangerous Branch: The Supreme Court at the Bar of Politics*, 1962.

3   The speech is published now as: 'Constitutional Reform and a Bill of Rights' [1997] EHRLR 483.

and views and cautioned that 'the Constitution is meant not only for people of their way of thinking but for all, and that the majority of the elected representatives of the people have, in authorising the imposition of the restrictions, considered them to be reasonable'.[4]

As we were reminded yesterday, the starting point of statutory interpretation is 'words'. The Supreme Court of South Africa said in 1990:

> The task of the courts is to ascertain from the words of the statute in the context thereof what the intention of the legislature is. If the wording of the statute is clear and unambiguous, they state what that intention is. It is not for the courts to invent fancied ambiguities and usurp the functions of the legislature.[5]

And, the Canadian Supreme Court has warned courts against invading the legislative field and substituting their views for that of the legislature.[6]

CONSTITUTIONAL INTERPRETATION

These rules of statutory interpretation must be used with care in relation to constitutional documents, because a constitution is drafted in broad and ample style and lays down principles of width and generality.[7] A constitution is made for generations to come.[8] Bhagwati J said in *People's Union for Democratic Rights v Union of India*:[9] 'The constitution-makers have given us one of the most remarkable documents in history for ushering in a new socio-economic order, and the Constitution that they have forged for us has a social purpose and a mission and therefore every word or phrase in the Constitution must be interpreted in a manner which would advance the socio-economic objectives of the Constitution.'

INTERPRETING A BILL OF RIGHTS

Common law rules of interpretation require skilful adaptation to deal with a Bill of Rights. As Lord Wilberforce reminded us in *Minister of Home Affairs v Fisher*, courts must avoid 'the austerity of tabulated legalism' and go for a generous and purposive interpretation suitable to give to individuals the full

---

4   *Indian Express Newspapers v Union of India* AIR 1986 SC 515, p 518.
5   *Government of the Republic of Bophuthatswana v Segale* 1990 (1) SA 434 (BA), p 448F–G.
6   *R v Andrews* [1989] 1 SCR 143, p 191.
7   *Minister of Home Affairs v Fisher* [1979] 3 All ER 21, p 25, *per* Lord Wilberforce.
8   'A constitution is framed for ages to come, and is designed to approach immortality as nearly as human institutions can approach it': *Cohens v Virginia*, 19 US (6 Wheat) 264, p 387, *per* Marshall CJ.
9   AIR 1982 SC 1473, p 1490.

measure of the fundamental rights and freedoms enshrined in the Constitution'. His Lordship treated Bermuda's Bill of Rights as *sui generis* calling for principles of interpretation of its own.

Generous and purposive

A Bill of Rights calls for a large and liberal interpretation for several reasons. For instance:

- a Bill of Rights uses general and imprecise language in order to lay down general principles that promote good governance. Specific legislation, such as for equal opportunities or privacy, may be enacted to implement the constitutional directives.

- Bills of Rights are greatly influenced by international treaties which are themselves expressed in general terms. Rights and freedoms recognised by international treaties transcend territorial boundaries. They acquire an international or universal meaning. It is common therefore to speak of 'autonomous meanings' that treaty words and phrases acquire.[10] These universal meanings have a profound influence on the interpretation of domestic Bills of Rights, although international tribunals generally recognise the need for 'a margin of appreciation'.[11]

- a Bill of Rights is generally directed to the government, to restrain government activity or to require government initiatives for the protection of individual rights.[12] Therefore, the traditional role of the judiciary as the citizen's protector is particularly decisive in the public sphere.

In interpreting a Bill of Rights which is binding on the legislature, what courts have to do is threefold:

- determine the scope of the rights and freedoms in keeping with the true spirit and objectives of the Constitution;[13]

---

10 Matscher, F, 'Methods of interpretation of the Convention', in Macdonald, R, Matscher, F and Petzold, H (eds), *The European System for the Protection of Human Rights*, 1993, pp 70–73.

11 *Ibid*, pp 75–78.

12 The Constitution of the Republic of South Africa, 1996, contains a very interesting provision:

> 8 (1) The Bill of Rights applies to all law, and binds the legislature, the executive, the judiciary and all organs of state.
>
> (2) A provision of the Bill of Rights binds a natural or a juristic person, if, and to the extent that, it is applicable, taking into account the nature of the right and the nature of any duty imposed by the right.

13 In *Ex parte Attorney General, Namibia in re Corporal Punishment by Organs of State*, 1991(3) SA 76, p 78A–C (Nam SC), it was said that the Namibian Constitution 'expresses the commitment of the Namibian people to the creation of a democratic society based on respect for human dignity, protection of liberty and the rule of law. Practices and values which are inconsistent with or which might subvert this commitment are vigorously rejected'.

- ascertain the legislative intention behind the statute alleged to be inconsistent with the constitutionally entrenched Bill of Rights; and
- decide the conflict between the constitutional purpose and legislative intention, one way or the other. In the end the Bill of Rights must prevail.

Interpretation clauses

In the interpretation of a Bill of Rights, the court may be assisted by an interpretation clause. For instance, section 39 of the 1996 Constitution of the Republic of South Africa provides as follows:

Interpretation of Bill of Rights

39(1) When interpreting the Bill of Rights, a court, tribunal or forum:

(a) must promote the values that underline an open and democratic society based on human dignity, equality and freedom;

(b) must consider international law; and

(c) may consider foreign law.

(2) When interpreting any legislation, and when developing the common law or customary law, every court, tribunal or forum must promote the spirit, purport and objectives of the Bill of Rights.

(3) The Bill of Rights does not deny the existence of any other rights or freedoms that are recognised or conferred by common law, customary law or legislation, to the extent that they are consistent with the Bill.

Limitations on fundamental rights

Fundamental rights are not absolute.[14] The American courts have evolved a number of implied restrictions on fundamental rights. It is the common practice in Commonwealth jurisdictions to specify limitations and restrictions in the Bill of Rights. An important task of the court is to decide whether a proposed restriction or limitation of a fundamental right or freedom can be accommodated within the relevant limitation clause or any implied limitation. Courts have insisted on strong justifications to permit any restriction of a fundamental right or freedom.[15]

---

14 Of course, a Bill of Rights may leave a fundamental right unaffected by any of the expressly stated limitations. Such a right, unless construed by courts to be subject to any implied limitation or qualification, must be regarded as absolute.

15 See *Handyside v UK* (1976) 1 EHRR 737 and *Young James and Webster v UK* (1982) 4 EHRR 38.

Value judgments and political questions

An important aspect of Bill of Rights interpretation is that judges are called upon to make value judgments, particularly when rights are in conflict. The conflict may be between two constitutionally protected rights, for example, the right to information and right to privacy, or between a constitutional right and a private right, for example, constitutionally protected freedom of expression and right to one's reputation protected by the law of tort or delict. The conflict assumes special importance when it is between a constitutionally protected right of an individual and a collective or community right. The court's decision favouring one conflicting right over the other, or harmonising them, is going to be criticised by one litigant party or the other on the ground that the court's decision is subjective, political or policy-laden.

In fact, it is generally accepted that the doctrine of political questions evolved by the American judiciary should not be used in human rights litigation. The argument is that human rights issues are by definition political issues.[16] The Namibia Supreme Court said in the *Re Corporal Punishment*[17] case:

> The decision which this court will have to make in the present case is based on a value judgment which cannot primarily be determined by legal rules and precedents, as helpful as they may be, but must take full cognisance of the social conditions, experiences and perceptions of the people of this country.

When courts take a pragmatic and cautious approach they will be criticised for not being 'brave enough'. When they take an exploratory and creative path there will be cries of 'save us from courts'.

SOME POINTS TO PONDER

In interpreting a Bill of Rights, courts have to take many matters into account, including the following:

(a) Are the rights and freedoms set out in the constitution exclusive, or are there unenumerated rights to be discovered and put into effect?[18]

(b) Since rights are entrenched as a safeguard against their intended or inadvertent breach by the government, the courts have to examine the

---

16 '... there seem to be very few exceptions to the general rule that the court will not apply the doctrine to the guarantees of the Bill of Rights': Scharpf, FW, 'Judicial review and political questions: a functional analysis' (1966) 75 Yale LJ 517, p 584.

17 *Ex parte Attorney General, Namibia in re Corporal Punishment by Organs of State*, 1991(3) SA 76 (Nam SC).

18 Australia does not have a Bill of Rights, but in recent years the High Court has held that the Constitution contains, by implication, a judicially enforceable commitment to fundamental freedoms. See Blackshield, T, Williams, G and Fitzgerald, B, *Australian Constitutional Law: Theory, Commentary and Materials*, Cap 21, 'Implied freedoms'.

purpose and antecedents of the relevant fundamental right, and the purpose and effect of the government action in question.

(c) What is the effect of a Bill of Rights? Does it have retrospective effect? Does it bind private actors in the absence of state action or state involvement? To what extent does a Bill of Rights affect the common law and customary laws?

(d) What is the relevance of human rights philosophy? For instance, how relevant is the apartheid background to a proper understanding of new constitutional regime in South Africa? Or, how do Directive Principles of State Policy help understand the meaning and scope of human rights in India?

(e) Should judges be wary of being too progressive or activist? In other words, how can they be innovative, but still not be viewed as confrontational?

(f) Are judges qualified by training and experience to handle human rights issues which have significant socio-political implications? Should there be extensive use of Brandeis brief-type investigative assistance?[19] Should there be special constitutional courts'?

These and many other issues will likely be identified in the course of our deliberations. And hopefully we will be able to identify some guiding principles for adoption at the end of our colloquium.

---

19 The Brandeis brief has its origin in *Muller v Oregon* 208 US 412 (1908). Brandeis brief type evidence to show the rational purpose of a law was used in the recent Canadian case of *Re RJR MacDonald Inc and Attorney General of Canada: Attorney General of Quebec, Intervener*, 1993 (102) DLR (4th) 289 (QCA).

CHAPTER 9

PARLIAMENTARY PRIVILEGE
VERSUS THE COURTS

Judge KM Nagabhushan Rao

Travelling all the way from *Ex parte Wason*[1] closely followed by *Church of Scientology v Johnson Smith*[2] to the ruling of Buckley J in *R v Currie* (1992, unreported), we have come a long way in solving the problem arising out of clashes between parliament and the courts as to their respective domains of power. Parliamentarians generally claim that what was said and what was done inside parliament is the exclusive domain of parliament and no outside agency has the power to interject. The basis for this contention is that members are exercising the sovereign and constitutional power of the public whom they represent and therefore their activities in parliament are not justiciable by institutions created by the Constitution.

On the other hand, over the years courts have taken the view that they have power to interfere for violation of the law. The logic behind their contention is that members of parliament can only have power and privileges in so far as their activities are legislative in nature and nothing beyond this. These rival contentions occasionally gave rise to a head-on collision between these two organs and remain unresolved.

The main element of contest between parliament and the courts is corruption of members of legislative bodies, something which the 'common law abhors' (*R v Whitaker*).[3] The champions of parliamentary privilege contend that even an allegation of corruption for any activity inside parliament is a breach of privilege and only the House is competent to deal with the matter and not the courts.

In fact, as early as 1695, the House of Commons resolved that the offer of money or other advantages to any member of parliament for promoting any matter whatsoever pending or to be transacted in the parliament is a high crime and misdemeanour. Those who advocate in favour of the power of interjection by the courts argue that since bribery is an offence at common law, the jurisdiction of the court to adjudicate cannot be ousted. Article 9 of the Bill of Rights 1688, stands as a stumbling block to the resolution of this dispute. The crucial question is whether protection given by this article can extend to cover any criminal activity under the guise of 'speech', 'debate', 'proceedings'

---

1   (1869) LR 4 QBD 573.
2   [1972] 1 All ER 378.
3   [1914] KB 1297.

in parliament or whether such activity attracts criminal proceedings outside parliament. This deadlock was sought to be solved by the Salmon Commission and Nolan Committee both of which took the view that members of parliament definitely do not fall within the criminal offence of corruption. The Salmon Commission recommended as follows:

> Parliament should consider bringing corruption, bribery and attempted bribery of members of parliament acting in their parliamentary capacity within the ambit of the criminal law. Our recommendation is limited to this single point and we do not raise any question of other aspects of parliamentary privileges and related matters.

The Nolan Committee called on the government to clarify the boundaries between the jurisdiction of parliament and the courts as follows:

> There is one area of conduct where a need already exists to clarify and perhaps alter, the boundary between courts and parliament. Bribery of members or the acceptance of the bribe is contempt of parliament and can be punished by the House ... It is quite likely that any members of parliament accepting bribes in connection with their parliamentary duties would be committing common law offences which could be tried by the courts. Doubt exists as to whether the courts or parliament have jurisdiction in such cases ... We believe that it would be unsatisfactory to leave this issue outstanding when other aspects of the law of parliament relating to conduct are being clarified. We recommend that the government should now take steps to clarify the law relating to bribery of or receipt of a bribe by a member of parliament.

Pursuant to the recommendations of the Nolan Committee, in 1996, the Home Office published a document entitled 'Clarification of The Law Relating to the Bribery of Members of Parliament' and invited the Select Committee on Standards and Privileges to consider four broad options:

(a) rely solely on parliamentary privilege to deal with accusations of bribery by members of parliament;

(b) subject members of parliament to the present corruption statute in full;

(c) distinguish between conduct which should be dealt with by the criminal law and that which should be left to parliament itself;

(d) make criminal proceedings subject to the approval of the relevant House of parliament.

The above problems are not confined to Great Britain alone and the impact is felt in other countries. For example, India has the largest parliamentary democracy in the world as well as an inherited Westminster pattern of governance after 1950. In India, the courts and the legislative bodies have clashed a number of times as evidenced in MSN Sharma's[4] case which was

---

4   *Pandit MSM Sharma v Shri Krishna Sinha and Others* (1959) Suppl 1 SCR 806.

closely followed by *Kesha v Singh*.[5] We had an historic opportunity of solving this problem in a recent case dealt with by the Supreme Court of India which is popularly known as the *JMM Bribery*[6] case. This case is unique in two respects:

(1) but for the switching sides by one judge out of five judges of the Constitutional Bench, it nearly resolved the deadlock which was constantly engaging the minds of legal luminaries throughout the Commonwealth; and

(2) it is the first time in history that a sitting Prime Minister, Sri PV Narasimha Rao, faced judicial scrutiny not only as a Prime Minister but also as a member of parliament, for his alleged act of bribing other members of parliament in order to get them to vote against the no-confidence motion which his government was facing.

Whenever a discussion takes place in India about the privileges of either members of parliament or members of the legislature, we are told that our members of parliament have the same privileges which are available to the members of the House of Commons. This brings us again to the original problem as to whether this is extended to cover criminal activities if they are committed inside parliament. The judgment of the Supreme Court dealt with the legal history of this problem in Great Britain, Canada, Australia and the USA. It analysed a number of judgments which led to the split of the Bench and the fifth judge switched over sides on two aspects. Thus we were dragged to the stage again of *Ex parte Wason*.

Briefly, the facts of the *JMM Bribery* case are as follows: the Prime Minister, along with some of his ministerial colleagues, Chief Ministers and members of parliament and some private persons were alleged to have bribed some members of parliament belonging to Jarkhand Mukti Morcha and other small groups in parliament to get their votes in order to defeat a no-confidence motion which was initiated by the opposition. On a public interest litigation, the Supreme Court directed the CBI, a leading investigative agency of the central government, to investigate the alleged bribery. A special court was constituted and when it took cognisance of the charges of bribery, the Prime Minister and others petitioned the High Court seeking an order to quash the proceedings. The High Court dismissed the proceedings and the matter went up to the Supreme Court. The charges were made under section 120B of the Indian Penal Code and under the Prevention of Corruption Act 1988.

The contentions of the accused were as follows:

(a) Even if the allegations of the prosecution were accepted, the court would have no jurisdiction to press charges for any criminal liability on the

---

5   Spl Reference No 1 of 1964 (1965) 1 SCR 412.
6   *PV Narasimha Rao v State* 1998 SC 626.

accused persons as whatsoever allegedly happened was in respect of votes given by some of them in the Lok Sabha (House of People) and that, in any case, whatever transpired, touched the privileges of the House within the meaning of Article 105(2) and (3) of the Constitution.

(b) Members of the Lok Sabha hold no office and as such were not public servants within the meaning of section 2(c) of the Prevention of Corruption Act 1988 and thus the Act would not apply to the alleged acts of omission and commission of the accused persons.

(c) Even if it could be taken that members of Lok Sabha did fall within section 2(c) of the Prevention of Corruption Act 1988, and were thus taken to be public servants, the Act would still not apply to members of the Lok Sabha as there was no authority competent to remove them from their office within the meaning of section 19(1)(c) of the Prevention of Corruption Act 1988.

The fact of bribes being given and taken was not in dispute in this case as one of the accused 'confessed' as to having taken the bribe for voting against the no-confidence motion. It must be remembered that Article 105 of the Constitution of India is nothing but the verbatim incorporation of the ruling of Cockburn, CJ and Blackburn, J in *Ex parte Wason* who held that anything said and done during the sitting of parliament was not impeachable outside the House. Previously in *R v AR Antuley*[7] the Supreme Court held that a member of the Legislative Assembly was not a public servant under section 21 of Indian Penal Code. But, the majority in the *JMM Bribery* case held that members of parliament are public servants for the purpose of the Prevention of Corruption Act. Unfortunately, one judge of the majority switched over to the minority when it came to the protection available under Article 105 of the Constitution and thus the opportunity to resolve this problem was missed. The minority view was broadly influenced by the Resolution of the House of Commons of 2 May 1695 that the 'offer of money or other advantage is a high crime and misdemeanour and tends subversion of the English Constitution'. The minority judges also considered an observation of Lord Salmon about the Bill of Rights, that 'a Charter of freedom of speech in the house is not a Charter for offence'. The minority of judges also heavily relied on the ruling of Buckley J in *R v Currie* that 'a member of parliament against whom there is a *prima facie* case of corruption should be immune from prosecution in the courts of law is to my mind an unacceptable proposition at the present time. I do not believe it to be the law'.

The position in Australia was also considered by the Supreme Court especially the ruling in *R v Wight*[8] which was approved by the High Court of Australia in *R v Boston*[9] in which the majority of the court held that the

---

7   1984 (2) SC 495.

8   13 SCR (NSW) 322.

9   (1923) 33 CLR 386.

protection available under Article 9 of the Charter would not cover a common law offence. However the third dissenting judge in the *Bribery* case favoured the dissenting judgments of Duffy and Starke JJ in the *Boston* case and thus joined the other two judges who said that Article 105 gave protection to the bribe-takers for their vote which was an activity that took place within the four walls of parliament. The Supreme Court also considered the Canadian position when Wilson CJ rejected the contention of protection for a crime by the defendant in *R v Bunting*.[10] However, the dissenting opinion of O'Connor J found favour with majority of the Supreme Court.

In the United States, the position is a little clearer in that the Supreme Court in *US v Brewster*[11] (by a majority) held that the 'speech and debate clause' only protected members of Congress from enquiry into legislative acts or into the motivation for their actual performance of legislative acts and it did not protect them from other activities they undertook that were political rather than legislative in nature. Further, that taking a bribe for the purpose of influencing one's official conduct is not part of any legislative process or function and the 'speech and debate clause' did not prevent indictment and prosecution of a legislator for accepting bribes. Even so, the majority of the Indian Supreme Court approved the dissenting judgment of Brennan and White JJ.

The conclusions of the Supreme Court judges in the *Bribery* case are as follows:

Per SC Agrawal J and Anand J

A 1 A member of parliament does not enjoy immunity under Article 105(2) or (3) of the Constitution from being prosecuted before a criminal court for an offence involving the offer or acceptance of a bribe for the purpose of speaking or by giving his/her vote in parliament or in any committees thereof.

   2 A member of parliament is a public servant under section 2(c) of the Prevention of Corruption Act 1988.

   3 Since there is no authority competent to remove a member of parliament and to grant sanction for his/her prosecution under section 19(1) of the Prevention of Corruption Act 1988, the court can take cognisance of the offences mentioned in section 19(1) in the absence of any other sanction. But until provision is made by parliament in that regard by suitable amendment to the law, the prosecuting agency, before filing a charge-sheet in respect of an offence punishable under sections 7, 10, 11, 13 and 15 of the Prevention of Corruption Act, against a member of parliament in a criminal court, shall obtain the permission of the Chairman of the Rajya Sabha/Speaker of the Lok Sabha as the case may be.

---

10 1884 (7) Ontario Reports 524.
11 33 L Ed 2d 507.

B   That on the basis of provisions of Article 105(2) and (3), the appellants could claim immunity from prosecution on the charges.

C   It would thus appear that, although in the Constitution the word 'office' had not been used in the provisions relating to members of parliament and members of state legislatures, in other parliamentary enactments relating to members of parliament, the word 'office' had been so used. Having regard to the provisions of the Constitution and the Representation of the People Act 1951 as well as the Salary, Allowance and Pension of Members of Parliament Act 1954 and the meaning given to the expression 'office' in decisions of the court, it was held that membership of parliament is an 'office' in as much as it is a position carrying certain responsibilities which are of a public character and it has an existence independent of the holder of the office. It must, therefore, be held that a member of parliament holds an 'office'.

D   That a member of parliament holds an office and by virtue of such office he/she is required or authorised to perform duties and such duties are in the nature of public duties. A member of parliament therefore falls within the ambit of section 2(c)(viii) of the Prevention of Corruption Act 1988.

Per GN RAY (partly dissenting)

E   I respectfully concur with the findings of Mr Justice Agrawal and agree with the reasoning for such findings that (1) a member of parliament is a public servant under section 2(c) of the Prevention of Corruption Act 1988, and (2) since there is no authority competent to grant sanction for the prosecution of a member of parliament under section 19(1) of the Prevention of Corruption Act 1988 the court can take cognisance of the offences mentioned in section 19(1) in the absence of any sanction, but before filing a charge sheet in respect of an offence punishable under the 1988 Act against a member of parliament in a criminal court, the prosecuting agency shall obtain the permission of the Chairman of the Rajya Sabha/Speaker of the Lok Sabha as the case may be. I have not been able to persuade myself to concur with the reasoning and the finding in the judgment of Mr Justice Agrawal that a member of parliament does not enjoy immunity under Article 105(2) or 105(3) of the Constitution from being prosecuted before a criminal court for an offence involving the offer or acceptance of a bribe for the purpose of speaking or giving his/her vote in parliament or in any committee thereof.

F   Therefore, an action impugned in a court proceeding which has a nexus with the vote cast or speech made in parliament must get protection under Article 105(2). Article 105(3) provides for other powers, privileges and immunities to be enjoyed by a member of parliament. The framers of the Constitution did not catalogue such powers, privileges and immunities but provided in Article 105(3) that, until such privileges are defined by the parliament, a member of parliament enjoys such powers, privileges and immunities which have been recognised to be existing for a member of House of Commons at the coming into force of the Constitution of India. I respectfully agree with the reasoning indicated in the judgment of my learned brother Mr Justice SP Bharucha that on the facts of the case, protection under Article 105(3) of the Constitution is not attacked but protection under of Article 105(2) is available only to those accused who, as members of parliament, had cast their votes in parliament.

Per SP Bharucha J (for himself and S Rajendra Babu J)

G Broadly interpreted, as it should be, Article 105(2) protects a member of parliament against proceedings in court that relate to, or concern, or have a connection or nexus with anything said, or a vote given, by him (or her) in parliament.

H The alleged bribe-takers, other than Ajit Singh, have the protection of Article 105(2) and are not answerable in a court of law for the alleged conspiracy and agreement. The charges against them must fail. Ajit Singh, not having cast a vote on the no-confidence motion, derives no immunity from Article 105(2).

I What is the effect of this upon the alleged bribe-givers? In the first place, the prosecution against Ajit Singh would proceed, for, by not having voted on the no-confidence motion, he does not enjoy the protection of Article 105(2). The charge against the alleged bribe-givers of conspiracy and agreement with Ajit Singh to do an unlawful act can therefore proceed.

J That the alleged bribe-takers who voted upon the no-confidence motion are entitled to the immunity conferred by Article 105(2).

K Accused nos 12 and 13 were at all relevant times private persons. The trial on all charges against them must proceed.

L When cognisance of the charges against them was taken, accused nos 7 and 9 were not public servants. The question of sanction for their prosecution, does not, therefore arise and the trial on all charges against them must proceed.

M Accused nos 1, 2, 8, 10, 11 and 14 (including PV Narasimha Rao) were public servants being either members of parliament or of a state legislature, when cognisance of the charges against them was taken. They were charged with substantive offences under section 120B of the Indian Penal Code and section 12 of the said Act. Since no prior sanction is required in respect of the charge under section 12 of the said Act, the trial on all charges against them must proceed.

N Accused no 15 was a public servant, being a member of parliament, when cognisance of the charges against him was taken. He is charged with substantive offences under section 120B of the Indian Penal Code and sections 7 and 13(2) of the said Act. The trial of the charge against him under section 120B of the Indian Penal Code must proceed.

From the above findings, it can be said that instead of distinguishing the activity of taking bribes even for a vote concerning normal legislative activity, the majority emphasised the place of incidence as important when it said that those members of parliament who took bribes and who voted accordingly were protected rather than those who gave the bribe. The protection given by the majority appears to be more for the sanctity of the House than for the nature of the activity and thus the majority view was criticised even in India by legal pundits on the ground that the majority considered the issue as a technicality and ignoring policy considerations.

CHAPTER 10

MAINTAINING JUDICIAL INDEPENDENCE IN A SMALL JURISDICTION

The Hon Chief Justice Derek Schofield

I should preface this paper by saying that my experience in small jurisdictions is limited to the Cayman Islands and Gibraltar both of which are British Overseas Territories each with a population of about 30,000. However, some of the problems which I shall discuss in the paper affect judges who are posted to a small town within a large jurisdiction. My experience is that the Cayman Islands and Gibraltar are jurisdictions where judges are not subjected to any direct interference in relation to the cases before them. There are stresses and strains particularly in maintaining the appearance or perception of independence but there are none of the problems of direct interference such as I encountered in my previous jurisdiction of Kenya. I should add that, unless the context suggests otherwise, when I speak of 'judges' I include those professional judges who preside in a court of law whether they be called judges or magistrates.

APPOINTMENTS

In both Gibraltar and the Cayman Islands, judges are appointed by the Governor who is himself appointed from the United Kingdom by Her Majesty the Queen. In Gibraltar, the appointment of Chief Justice and the Judges of Appeal are made on instructions given by Her Majesty through the Secretary of State for Foreign and Commonwealth Affairs. In the Cayman Islands, the appointment of the Chief Justice and the Judges of Appeal are made with the approval of the Secretary of State. Magistrates in both jurisdictions are appointed by the Governor acting at his/her own discretion. In practice, the Governor will consult the Chief Justice before making any judicial appointment.

Clearly, in making appointments the Governor will wish to take account of local sensitivities. These may manifest themselves in two ways: (a) a desire to see local persons appointed to senior positions; and (b) a desire to have local participation in the appointment process. Sometimes, it is difficult to reconcile the desire for the appointment of a local person to a judicial position with the necessity to appoint someone with impartiality or perceived impartiality when one is drawing from a population of 30,000. Lord Bingham has said:

> The key to successful making of appointments must, I would suggest, lie in an assumption shared by appointor, appointee and public at large that those appointed should be capable of discharging their judicial duties, so far as humanly possible, with impartiality. Impartiality and independence may not, even in this context, be synonyms, but there is a very close blood-tie between them: for a judge who is truly impartial, deciding each case on its merits as they appear to him (or, of course, her), is of necessity independent.[1]

In a small jurisdiction, an individual is known by a large majority of the population. Family connections may be quite extensive in a small community. The judge may have grown up in a close proximity to the very people he/she would, as a judge, be called upon to try. By the time the person is ready to take up a judicial appointment, he/she may have formed allegiances, social, professional and political. These are known throughout the length and breadth of a small community. Lawyers tend to become rather vocal politically and are often seen to be aligned to a particular political grouping. Lawyers are reluctant to join a service which attracts modest remuneration. Able lawyers can earn substantially more in private practice than a government with limited means can afford to pay, and indeed practitioners who are often the most suitable candidates for an appointment to preside in the criminal courts are those who have built up a substantial practice at the criminal Bar. They are thus more likely to meet their former clients if they are to sit as a judge. It is the exceptional individual who emerges as both willing and able to perform the functions of a judge in technical and personal terms. If that exceptional individual does emerge then he/she must be the favoured candidate. However, that bias in favour of a local appointee should not lead to the appointment of an unsuitable candidate.

The tendency in some jurisdictions is to recruit almost wholly or substantially from overseas. There now seems to have grown a practice of advertising judicial posts and conducting an open competition, the Governor appointing a board to interview those who are short-listed. This is to be commended whether there are local candidates or not. It is vital that only the best candidates are recruited for judicial positions. Furthermore, an open recruitment system lends credibility to an appointment and stems possible criticism that an appointment is made other than on merit.

To what extent should the Governor consult locally on appointments? The Governor is, of course, the head of the executive but is removed from local politics. It will be natural for the incumbent to want to pass across the other members of the executive the name of a potential appointee particularly if the potential appointee is or should be known to the members of the executive, if only to ascertain if there is anything known about that person which ought to

---

1   The Rt Hon Lord Bingham of Cornhill, Lord Chief Justice of England, Lecture on Judicial Independence delivered to the English Judicial Board on 5 November 1996.

be taken into consideration. But, the members of the executive are elected politicians who in a small jurisdiction will be all too familiar with a local candidate. It is not like a large jurisdiction where such matters can be dealt with impersonally; in a small jurisdiction matters tend to become personalised.

My view is that it is right and proper for the Governor to inform the other members of the executive about a prospective appointment, but that he or she should not go so far as to formally consult. The dividing line between formal consultation and requesting formal approval is too fine, and in a small jurisdiction it would be dangerous for the politicians to become part of the formal appointment process to the judiciary.

SECURITY OF TENURE

Sir Gerard Brennan has said:

> Independence of the modern judiciary has many facets. The external factors that tend to undermine independence are well recognised by the judiciary but perhaps not so well recognised by the political branches of government or by the public. Some of the structures that preserve independence are well established. I need not canvass the twin constitutional pillars of independence – security of tenure and conditions of service that the executive cannot touch – except to say this: if either of these pillars is eroded, in time, society will pay an awful price.[2]

In Gibraltar and the Cayman Islands, for the judges, the usual provisions relating to tenure and removal from office are written into the Constitution. In both Territories, the same provisions also exist for protection of magistrates.

On the death of the Colonial Legal Service, with its structure and security for officers within it, there grew up a system of appointment and contract of officers recruited from overseas. It seems furthermore that the contract system has not, in some jurisdictions, been confined to expatriate judges. A fixed term contract and security of tenure for judges do not reconcile, because a judge does not know whether unpopular decisions are going to rebound upon him/her when the time comes for renewal of contract. There are dangers that those affected by a judge's decisions will be tempted to try to influence the Governor's decision whether to renew the contract of a judge. For example, members of government may be sensitive to decisions on judicial review. For this reason, I consider the Governor ought to limit the consultative process on renewal more rigorously even than is done on the appointment of judges.

---

2   The Hon Sir Gerard Brennan, Chief Justice of Australia to the Australian Judicial Conference, 2 November 1996.

Furthermore, where a judge seeks to renew his/her contract, a renewal should only normally be refused on grounds of inability to discharge the functions of office or where the judge has been guilty of misbehaviour during the currency of the contract. Perhaps added to these grounds in the case of an expatriate judge is where a local candidate for the post has emerged with all the necessary technical and personal attributes. A judge should, furthermore, be entitled to be given reasons for non-renewal of contract.

I should say, of course, that the instability that the system of contracts for judges brings is not confined to small jurisdictions. The only time I was threatened that renewal of my contract was in jeopardy was in Kenya where I was told by the then Chief Justice that, if I persisted in dealing with a particular case in a particular way, he would have difficulty recommending a renewal. I ought to add for the record that I informed the Chief Justice that if that was the price I had to pay for a renewal of contract I was not prepared to pay it. However, small jurisdictions are particularly susceptible to the kind of dangers demonstrated in this section of the paper. Cases take on a local magnitude, often far in excess of their importance. Personal reasons are often attributed to perfectly sound decisions and it is easy for a judge to become labelled, as, say, anti-government on the basis of one or two decisions. I suspect that, if judges on contract were asked whether, when renewal time comes around, they ask themselves if they have made any unpopular decisions, many would reply in the affirmative.

It may be that a judge recruited from an overseas territory does not want to be committed to the jurisdiction until retirement age. It may be that the recruiting territory does not want to commit itself to an expatriate judge until retirement age, particularly in a small jurisdiction where some provision ought to be made for the emergence of local candidates for the very few judicial posts available. Furthermore judges from overseas are very much an unknown quantity and it is often uncertain whether they will fit within the local perceptions of judicial conduct. It may be that the contract system is, therefore, a necessary evil. But, it is an evil which ought to be contained better within the written law or within the terms of the contracts themselves, by more rigorous provisions in favour of judges who seek renewal of their contract.

RELATIONS WITH THE EXECUTIVE

The judiciary cannot operate independently of the executive. As Lord Bingham has pointed out:

> After appointment, judges sit in courts provided by the state, they have offices provided, heated and lighted by the state, they have clerks paid by the state,

they use books and computers mostly provided by the state, they are themselves paid by the state.[3]

The money available to the courts has to be provided by the executive and in theory at least the executive could express its displeasure with the judiciary by denying it the necessary funds. In practice, that has never happened in either Gibraltar or in the Cayman Islands, so far as I am aware. Perhaps problems in this area are brought into sharper focus in small jurisdictions with smaller budgets where there is a tendency for small budgetary matters to be subject to central control. For example, if I require the funds to attend a conference, the Registrar has to submit an application to the Chief Secretary. In theory, the Chief Secretary, or whoever is consulted, could prevent me from attending a conference if it was considered that it was inappropriate for me to do so, either because of the contents of the programme of the conference or because of what I was likely to say. But, these are perceptions of possible ways of interfering with the activities of members of the judiciary and I cannot imagine being denied funding on those grounds. In practice, it will be a question of whether funds are available.

In my experience in both Gibraltar and the Cayman Islands, the courts are adequately funded within the budgetary constraints of the respective governments. Similarly with staffing. With good will and a sensible approach on both sides, the courts are reasonably adequately manned. There is a provision in the Gibraltar Supreme Court Ordinance which, in theory, permits the Chief Justice to determine the number of officers required to carry out the administration of the court. In practice, the Registrar of the Supreme Court deals with staffing matters directly with the Personnel Department of government, in the same way as government departments. It would only be if the Registry were to become dangerously understaffed that the Chief Justice would enter the staffing arena and wield the statutory provision above-mentioned.

The Registrar and Deputy Registrar of the Supreme Court of Gibraltar, according to section 3 of the Supreme Court Ordinance, are 'attached and belong to the court'. These officers are, of course, provided by the government but are appointed by the Governor. They carry out some judicial duties as well as being responsible for the administration of the court. A few years ago a Registrar was removed on the directions of the then Chief Minister and transferred to the Attorney General's Chambers. How this came about in the face of the statutory provision I do not know. I can only assume that it was an aberration which would not be repeated today. In Gibraltar, members of staff other than the Registrar and Deputy Registrar can be transferred to and from the courts at the will of the administration. In theory, this could lead to problems and conflict. There could, for example, in theory, be an attempt by a

---

3   Lord Bingham, above, fn 1.

senior member of the administration to influence a listing officer concerning the allocation of a particular case, with a refusal resulting in some form of reprisal. In practice, the registries have been permitted to maintain and develop a nucleus of able and senior staff whose allegiance is to the court rather than to the administration and who are well versed in the intricacies of procedure and language of the courts.

In many jurisdictions, judges appear to have difficulty in getting across to the administration that judicial salaries need to be high enough to attract suitable candidates and the judge's role is such that it cannot, for remuneration purposes, be equated to or compared with administrative positions. In a small jurisdiction, there is a danger that it will be the relations between the particular post-holder and those holding the purse-strings which will determine levels of remuneration and allowances rather than considerations of principle.

MAINTAINING PROFESSIONAL INTEGRITY

It is necessary for the proper administration of justice for judges to maintain the respect of the Bar. They should do so on a professional and social level. For this reason, it is essential for judges to keep abreast of the law and current judicial trends and to conduct themselves in their private lives in a manner which preserves the dignity of their office.

On the first point, it must, to a large extent, be left to the individual judge to keep up-to-date. A small jurisdiction does not have the facilities or the personnel to offer the kind of judicial training now available, and often compulsory, in some large jurisdictions, at least so far as the superior court judges are concerned. In both Gibraltar and the Cayman Islands, there is occasional training of Justices of the Peace, usually conducted by a judge or stipendiary magistrate. But facilities do not exist for the training of the professional judges.

The facilities offered by the English Judicial Studies Board to judges of the Commonwealth are therefore extremely valuable. The Commonwealth Judicial Education Institute should also be mentioned in this connection. It is important that judges from jurisdictions which do not provide judicial training have an opportunity to undertake such training. Furthermore, training courses give judges from small jurisdictions which are starved of contact with judicial brethren an opportunity to make such contact. The importance of this latter element can probably only be fully appreciated by those who are judges in small jurisdictions.

I shall deal with the general social problems encountered by a judge in the next section of the paper, but here I deal with social relations with members of the Bar. One tends to gravitate socially towards people with similar backgrounds. However, in a small jurisdiction, there are no Inns of Court to retreat to. One's social life tends to become common knowledge. The Bar, particularly the litigation Bar, is very small. There are those members of the Bar to whom one is naturally attracted; it cannot be ignored that there are sometimes members of the Bar who seek to ingratiate themselves to the judges. Too close a contact with any particular member of the Bar may give a wrong impression to the other members of the Bar and, particularly, to the public. Too close a contact with the Attorney General or any members of his/her chambers may also be misconstrued. For this reason, a judge in a small jurisdiction has to maintain a reserve which leads to a very lonely existence.

SOCIAL PRESSURES

This latter consideration applies equally to a judge's general social activities. We all need friends and social contact but the chances of meeting a litigant in a social context is multiplied in a small jurisdiction. Anonymity is lost and the burden of maintaining the dignity of the office is often great. It is not good for one's office for one to be perceived to be out of touch with society and there are official gatherings which a judge is expected to attend. On the other hand, one does not want to be readily approachable for fear of attracting the wrong approach. For my part, my experience tells me that if I have to choose between appearing remote and appearing approachable, I prefer the former.

Much of a judge's official social life in a small jurisdiction requires interaction with officials who are potential or actual litigants. He/she may have spent the day hearing an application for judicial review against a decision of the Governor and in the evening be expected to attend the Governor's residence to meet an official guest. Every time a judge ventures outside, there is a likelihood of meeting someone who he/she has had to find against or even someone who he/she has previously sent to prison. For my part, I have never been or even felt threatened, but I could recount many instances when I have been made to feel uncomfortable.

There is another element to this problem. It is right and proper that a judge's decisions should be open to public and press comment and even criticism. In a small jurisdiction, it is the same small number of judges who are making the decisions. Often, matters which are everyday occurrences in a larger jurisdiction are sensational news in a smaller jurisdiction. In this way, a judge's decisions can press upon him/her in a way which judges in larger jurisdictions do not experience. There is little chance of escape. And, it is not inappropriate to mention here the added burden of discretion placed on a judge's spouse and family.

For all these reasons, there is much to be said for the system of providing judges in small jurisdictions (and other senior officers for that matter) with housing in a private complex or area. One may not particularly want to have the Attorney General, the Commissioner of Police or the Chief Secretary as one's neighbour, but they are preferable to some other neighbours one could have. In Gibraltar and in the Cayman Islands, there has been a tendency for the government to attempt to rid itself of these 'institutional' houses. To leave judges to have to go on the open market for housing, particularly when salaries or allowances can lead them to inferior accommodation in less desirable areas of their jurisdiction, is an unwelcome policy.

Finally, I should mention one particular problem in a small jurisdiction in maintaining impartiality on the Bench. Every jurisdiction has its recidivists. Every jurisdiction has its regular litigants who may not have achieved the description 'vexatious'. In a small jurisdiction, such clients appear before the same judge or judges. There is little possibility of such a client appearing before a judge who has not already found against them. It often takes an extreme effort on the part of the judge to deal with such a client impartially. We all do it but all know the amount of effort it takes.

It is in society's best interests that protective barriers be erected behind which judges will be free to fulfil their judicial functions independently and impartially. But, however secure those barriers, it is for individual judges, whether sitting in a small or a larger jurisdiction, to maintain their own standards of judicial conduct. As Lord Hope has said:

> The responsibility lies with the judiciary to ensure that it is not weakened by the actions of the executive, or by incautious or irresponsible conduct on the part of the judiciary. At the end of the day, what matters most is the extent to which the judges themselves value and assert their own independence and foster it by their traditions and conduct. The terms and conditions of service provide a framework upon which that independence can be built. But, the real substance of independence lies in the hearts and minds of the judges and the way in which from day to day they administer justice.[4]

---

4 Lord Hope of Craighead, Address on 'Human Rights and Judicial Independence' to the Commonwealth Magistrates' and Judges' Association Meeting, Cape Town, South Africa, 1997.

CHAPTER 11

ROLE OF NON-JUDICIAL AND NON-PARLIAMENTARY INSTITUTIONS: THE PRACTISING LEGAL PROFESSION

Cyrus V Das

INTRODUCTION

It is a daunting task to speak of the legal profession in the midst of a profound debate on the role of parliament, the executive and the judiciary. Lawyers are protean characters. They flit in and out of all segments of government almost effortlessly as if they were Plato's ideal of schooled-leaders. But it is not the lawyer as an individual that we are concerned with, but rather the proper role of their Bar Association in the overall development of constitutionalism and the rule of law in society.

THE BAR ASSOCIATION IN A DEVELOPED AND DEVELOPING SOCIETY

I venture to suggest that a dichotomy exists in the perception and perspective of the role of the Bar Association in a developed and developing society. It is no less with regard to what is perceived as a threat to judicial independence in different societies. Joshua Rosenberg in his recent book, *Trial By Strength*,[1] wrote of the removal of the sentencing discretion of judges in the United Kingdom as the basis of the complaint that the former Conservative government took measures that resulted in an erosion of judicial independence in the country. Speaking of this in the debate in the House of Lords, and later in a public lecture, Lord Ackner[2] said:

> Currently there is much controversy concerning the Home Secretary's proposal to be found in the Crime (Sentences) Bill relative to minimum sentences and mandatory life sentences. The essential complaint by the judiciary is that there would be cases in which these proposals would prevent the judges from doing justice. Indeed, there would be occasions in which they would be obliged to do injustice ... I conclude by going back 20 years to the first international conference of appellate judges held in Manila and I end with a quotation from the then Lord President – that is the Chief Justice of Malaysia

1 Rosenberg, J, *Trial by Strength: The Battle between Ministers and Judges over who makes the Law*, 1997.
2 Ackner (Lord), 'The erosion of judicial independence' (1996) 140 NLJ 1789, p 1791.

– Tun Mohamed Suffian, an old friend of mine and a fellow bencher of Middle Temple, who warned delegates to be on their guard: 'because ... while all governments publicly endorse the principle, some quietly work to undermine it, and it behoves judges of the world to be on their guard against the erosion of their independence'.

But, the fixation of minimum and mandatory sentences in penal statutes is commonplace in many developing countries. It would not by itself be seen as destructive of judicial independence. We may by contrast see the more profound fears expressed by Muhammad Habibur Rahman J of the Bangladesh Supreme Court on the subject of judicial independence:

> For developing countries, no uniform judicial role can be fashioned out. In some of the developing countries, the very existence of the judiciary as an institution is at stake. In that unenviable condition, the primary role of a judge will be, if he does not decide to leave his post, to hold on. If he fails to roar like a lion, it is understandable. If he keeps a glum face and gives a withering look then that will be good work. For the time being, the worthwhile role for him will be to do justice between a citizen and a citizen, so that a foundation may be laid for the future when a citizen will be able to expect justice against the mighty and the overbearing as well. In the present day world, there are bad omens and good auguries. In some societies, rays of early dawn are chasing away the darkness.[3]

Thus, it is not surprising that definitions of judicial independence vary with the experience of society and its judges. Chief Justice Gibbs of Australia was able to define the term in a rather uncomplicated way:

> It means that no judge should have anything to hope or fear in respect of anything which he or she may have done properly in the course of performing judicial functions. So neither the parliament nor the executive, nor anyone else, should be able to bring pressure of any kind to bear upon a judge in the performance of judicial duties.[4]

In comparison, the definition attempted by Justice HR Khanna of the Indian Supreme Court had perforce to be elaborate reflecting all the polemics and controversies that go with the term in a developing society:

> And while talking of the independence of courts, I must remove a misconception. Independence of courts does not necessarily mean deciding a case against the State. Sometimes, a notion prevails that the more a judge decides cases against the State, the more independent he (or she) is. This is a wholly misleading notion and the sooner it is dispelled the better it is for the health of the community ... Every government in a welfare state has to undertake a number of measures with a view to bringing about socio-

---

3   Quoted from the writer's, *Government and Crisis: A Study Of The Use Of Emergency Powers*, 1996, p 400.

4   Sturges, G and Chubb, P, *Judging The World: Law And Politics In The World's Leading Courts*, 1988, p 353.

economic reforms ... The modern approach is that the welfare of the community must have primacy over the private rights of the individual. We, therefore, should not take a lopsided view of the independence of the judiciary. Independence postulates keeping the scales even in any legal combat between the rich and the poor, the mighty and the weak, the State and the citizen. As much injustice can be done by keeping the scales weighted in favour of the citizen and against the State, as it can be by keeping the scales weighted in favour of the State and against the citizen.[5]

The definition reflects the experience of developing nations that have adopted the Westminster model. It shows a continuing accommodation being sought between the three organs of State especially in the role of the judiciary as the arbiter of disputes with the State. In some nations the experiment has failed, reflected most poignantly in a take-over by the military. In others, the efforts at accommodation continues. I would suggest that it is in this arena of building constitutionalism and meeting the challenges of the socio-economic aspirations of the people that the role of a Bar Association would vary according to its locus in a developing or developed society.

At the foremost is the need in an underdeveloped or developing country for an independent Bar.

THE IMPORTANCE OF AN INDEPENDENT BAR[6]

It is axiomatic that lawyers are vital cogs in the machinery of justice, and unless there is an independent Bar ready and willing to defend rights that are guaranteed in society there cannot truly be said to be freedom and the rule of law. Lord Alexander of Weedon, QC, in an address to the Malaysian Bar in 1991, said:

Without a democratic society you cannot have an independent legal system and an independent legal profession. But without such a system of law and such a profession to practice the law, you cannot have true democracy. So democracy and the law are twin pillars of a free society.

It is in the role of aiding the administration of justice in a civilised society that the first and foremost role of an independent Bar may be seen. Lord Macmillan, a distinguished Law Lord, described this function in its context as follows:[7]

Ever since the State decreed that men must cease to settle their disputes with the arguments of fist and club, the administration of justice has been the prime

---

5   Khanna, HR, *Law, Men of Law and Education*, 1981, p 9.
6   This part is taken from a Memorandum for the Malaysian Bar prepared by the writer, see INSAF (Journal of the Malaysian Bar) Vol XXV (no 3) July 1996, p 1 *et seq*.
7   See Macmillan (Lord), *Law and Other Things*, 1938, p 173.

concern of the State. In order to enable this primary function of government to be efficiently discharged, the experience of every civilised community has shown that it is indispensable to have a class of men skilled in advising and aiding the citizen in the vindication of rights before the courts to which the State delegates the task of dispensing justice in accordance with the law of the land.

The justice system cannot function without an independent judiciary which is able to administer justice impartially. In turn, an independent judiciary cannot exist without an independent Bar. Lord Macmillan continued:[8]

> For it has long been proved that the most effectual and only practicable method of arriving at the rights of a dispute is by critical debate in the presence of an impartial third party, where every statement and argument on either side is submitted to the keenest scrutiny and attack. Where every step on the way to judgment has been tested and contested, the chance of error in the ultimate decision is reduced to a minimum. The better the case is presented on each side, and the keener and more skilful the debate before him, the more likely is it that the judge will reach a just and sound judgment. *That is why it has been said that a strong Bar makes a strong bench. It is, then, as contributing an essential element to the process of the administration of justice that the profession of the advocate discharges a public function of the highest utility and importance.* [My emphasis.]

Echoing similar sentiments, Mahajan CJ of the Indian Supreme Court said in an address in 1954:[9]

> ... a strong Bar and a strong judiciary are a *sine qua non* for the maintenance of the rule of law. It is the Bar that makes both the Ministry and the judiciary go straight. If the Bar becomes a mere money-making machine, then it will be failing in its duty towards the nation.

Fearless advocacy is not possible without the guarantee to the lawyer of independence and freedom from reprisal. Speaking of this, Mohd Qarim Chagla CJ of the Bombay High Court has said:[10]

> Great advocacy must be both fearless and fair. The administration of justice is made possible not only by a fair and impartial judge, but also by a courageous and upright advocate ... The Bar is one of the most important of all professions. Those who join it belong to a great fraternity. *The most valuable assets they enjoy are complete independence and integrity.* [My emphasis.]

Speaking on the same theme, Lord Alexander has emphasised that, without this independence, lawyers would decline to take up an unpopular cause in society or represent an unpopular client:[11]

---

8   See *op cit*, Macmillan, fn 7, pp 175–76.
9   See Sarkar, R, *Modern Advocacy*, 1985, p 83.
10   See his *Autobiography*, 1978, pp 70 and 72–73.
11   Address to the Malaysian Bar, 1991.

These basic duties explain why it is so important that society should respect the independence of the advocate. This independence has been traditionally regarded throughout the common law as fundamental. It enables the advocate to resist all pressures in an unpopular cause, and to present the case without fear or favour. *Without this independence, there would be no effective rule of law and the basic duty of the advocate to protect the rights and liberties of the citizen could not be fulfilled.* [My emphasis.]

Is the unpopular cause to be consigned away and the unpopular client to be condemned unrepresented? Neither would lawyers without the guarantee of independence take up cases against powerful organisations or the Establishment. As a former chairman of the Malaysian Bar, Raja Aziz Addruse has put it:[12]

In the performance of their professional duties as a lawyer, members of the Bar may find themselves having to represent their clients against influential personalities, powerful organisations and even the Establishment; and if they are to do justice by their clients, they must be prepared, and are, by rules of conduct and etiquette applicable to them, enjoined to undertake their duties without fear or favour. *The need for lawyers to act without fear or favour in advocating their client's cause is evident if one considers the nature of their profession.* [My emphasis.]

In addition, the legal profession as a body has a societal role to play. It falls upon it to identify the shortcomings in legislation or governmental action from the standpoint of civil rights. The stand it takes may not be popular and may well be misunderstood. But it does not behove a Bar Council to take popular stands as opposed to a stand that is in accordance with justice. Of these matters, a leading Malaysian sociologist, Chandra Muzaffar wrote and emphasised the importance of an independent Bar:[13]

Law as a profession has always been concerned with the position of the State, its constitution, its law and what they imply for the well being of the man-in-the-street. By the same token, the profession has, since its genesis, been deeply immersed in questions pertaining to the rights and responsibilities of the individual. Inevitably, the pursuit of human rights – whether it is the right to fair compensation or to fair wages or to liberty – must result in conflict with certain interests in society. Sometimes these interests are protected by the state; sometimes the state itself is the interested party. Lawyers who value their profession will not desist from the conflict simply because it involves the State. They will not argue that the Bar Council as a professional body should not be dragged into 'politics'. For they will realise that it is the duty of a professional body to defend those rights which are the *raison d'etre* of the profession itself. Lawyers do not cease to be lawyers the moment the law concerned compels them to confront the powers-that-be.

---

12 See [1983] 2 CLJ 181.
13 See [1983] 2 CLJ 231.

In the same vein, it falls upon the Bar Association to advise and comment on legislation touching on the legal, personal and property rights of citizens and their liberties. Indeed no organisation is better placed to discharge this function than the Bar. This function cannot be discharged meaningfully unless the Bar is independent and is free to comment without fear of reprisal or penalty.

An independent legal profession is vital to economic progress and development. Unless investors are confident that they may resort to an independent and non-aligned Bar for advice and representation in their disputes with any party, no matter how powerful or well connected they may be, investors' confidence is likely to deteriorate. As Lord Alexander said, speaking of Malaysia's economic progress:[14]

> The ability to conduct trade, within the boundaries of law, and to know that a settled system of law is available to resolve differences, is crucial to economic progress. The economic progress made within your country within recent years, with improved opportunities for employment and higher standards of living, is most good to see. Your system of law, and your professional work, are not just an adjunct grafted on to the commerce of society, but an essential element in its development. Legal rights do not impede economic progress: they buttress it.

THE PUBLIC ROLE OF THE BAR

These quotations speak eloquently of a public role for lawyers and their Bar Associations. The experience of the developed nations show the defining role played by lawyers in the early constitutional development of their countries. In the USA, the visiting French writer de Tocqueville was able to say of the contributions of American lawyers of the last century that:

> ... they form the highest political class and the most cultivated section of society. If I am asked where I place the American aristocracy I should reply without hesitation ... that it occupies the judicial bench or bar.[15]

That may be disputed today, but even then over the last half century or so in the USA who can ignore the role of lawyers in the struggle for civil rights emancipation long after the Lincoln proclamation. *Brown v Board of Education* (347 US 483 (1954)) was the culmination of a struggle led by lawyers under the leadership of Thurgood Marshall (later a Justice of the Supreme Court) and the NAACP (National Association for the Advancement of Coloured People).

But we must not ignore the converse; that of the appalling catastrophe of omission and complicity in the face of state-operated cruelty and brutality.

---

14 See fn 11, above.
15 Quoted in Khanna, *op cit*, fn 5, p 15.

Muller in his book *Hitler's Justice*[16] details the failing of the German legal system and personages during the madness of the Third Reich. The easy conformist approach taken by some local Bar Associations under Hitler's Reich was illustrated by the author when he quoted the President of the Dresden Bar Association who 'stressed the struggle of genuine German attorneys true to the German view of the profession against liberal Jewish attitudes in legal life and that an attorney's duty to his client is limited by his duties towards his society', thereby effectively calling for abolition of the profession's freedom and independence.[17] Goldhagan in his recent best seller *Hitler's Willing Executioners* wrote of the complicity of the German legal community in these terms:

> Judges and members of the legal profession were so eager to purge their institutions and their country of Jewish influence that they, beginning already in the first few months of Nazi governance, often outran the legal mandates that the regime promulgated.[18]

These are some of the experiences of the developed countries on their road to a stable constitutional system. In today's environment, the greatest need for vigilance and a public role for the Bar is in the underdeveloped or developing countries. The developed countries invariably have a sufficient number of independent watchdog bodies with clout and resources to monitor and enforce the status of civil liberties in their society. Examples abound but to mention some: Amnesty International, Inter-Rights and the American Civil Liberties Union.

In less developed countries, the Bar plays the role of the guardian of the judiciary and of civil rights. The character and ethos of every society is different. The choice of method and strategy to advance the cause of constitutionalism so that people live in a free and democratic society is best left to the local Bar to determine.

At the foremost must be the pro bono culture. The best at the Bar must be available to advocate crucial and hard cases pivotal to basic freedoms. A strong culture along these lines does prevail at many of the established Bars. Can we forget the famous story of *Gideon v Wainright*[19] in the US Supreme Court that established the basic right of every indigent accused person to be defended by counsel. The case was argued in the Supreme Court as a pro bono case by Abe Fortas, then a leading and expensive advocate at the Washington Bar. His preparation and commitment to the case was so great

---

16 Muller, I, *Hitler's Justice: The Courts of the Third Reich*, 1991.

17 See above. It is fair to mention that Muller records several instances of courageous stands taken by German judges and attorneys who refused to conform to Nazism and paid the price of ostracisation in service.

18 Goldhagan, DJ, *Hitler's Willing Executioners: Ordinary Germans and The Holocaust*, p 97.

19 372 US 335.

that Justice William O Douglas was later to remark that it was amongst the best argument he had ever heard in the Supreme Court.[20] There can be no better praise of a Bar than that.

In developing societies, the legal profession invariably enjoys a standing and influence that enables its views to be heard by government. Bar associations must seize this fact to state their opinions, to articulate their concerns and to advocate their cause for a civil society where individual liberties are guaranteed under a system of constitutional government. The technique, approach and method would necessarily vary given the circumstance of each society.

In some extreme cases, the remedy has not been within the system, for example, of Tilak and Gandhi before the British colonial courts for sedition, or Nelson Mandela before the apartheid court for treason.[21] But in the vast number of cases, the Bar Association that espouses values and principles of justice enjoys a public standing that assures it of an audience in the right places and a solicitous consideration of its views. There is room for confidence that Daniel Webster's declamation 'the power of the clear statement is the great power of the Bar' holds true today even a century later.

---

20 Douglas, WO, *The Court Years*, 1981, p 187.

21 Repudiation of the system occurs where the enforcing authority lacks moral or legal legitimacy to govern. Mandela at his treason trial challenged the authority of the court in these words: 'I challenge the right of this court to hear my case in a political trial, such as this one, which involves the clash of the aspirations of the African people and those of Whites. The country's courts as presently constituted, cannot be impartial and fair; what sort of justice is this that enables the aggrieved to sit in judgment over those against whom they have laid a charge?': Mandela, N, *No Easy Walk To Freedom*, 1965, p 126.

CHAPTER 12

PARLIAMENTARIANS, NATIONAL INSTITUTIONS AND THE IMPLEMENTATION OF THE HARARE COMMONWEALTH DECLARATION

John Hatchard

Devising strategies for strengthening the democratic framework within Commonwealth jurisdictions in the context of the Harare Commonwealth Declaration, 1991, and Millbrook Commonwealth Action Programme on the Harare Declaration, 1995, is multi-faceted. Whilst the relationship between the executive, legislature and judiciary inevitably takes centre stage, human rights commissions and offices of the ombudsman (hereinafter referred to collectively as 'national institutions') can also provide significant support for the democratic process. This paper argues that, in this respect, their relationship with parliament is an important one in that, on the one hand, parliament can support and strengthen the operation of national institutions whilst on the other, national institutions can assist parliamentarians through providing objective advice and information relating to proposed legislation and the promotion and protection of human rights.

The paper is divided into four sections. The first provides an overview of national institutions in the Commonwealth; the second explores the support role parliament can provide vis à vis such institutions; the third examines the contribution of such institutions to the work of parliamentarians; whilst the final section provides a brief overview.

NATIONAL INSTITUTIONS IN THE COMMONWEALTH

National institutions are statutory bodies and traditionally are divided generally into offices of the ombudsman and human rights commissions.[1] The 1974 resolution of the International Bar Association sets out concisely the traditional functions of an ombudsman:

> An office provided for by the constitution or by action of the legislature or parliament and headed by an independent high-level public official who is responsible to the legislature or parliament, who receives complaints from

---

1   See, generally, Hatchard, J (ed), *National Human Rights Institutions in the Commonwealth: Directory and Analysis,* Commonwealth Secretariat, 1992.

aggrieved persons against government agencies, officials and employees or who acts on his/her own motion, and who has the power to investigate, recommend corrective action and issue reports.[2]

Offices of the ombudsman operate today in some 35 Commonwealth countries.

In the Harare Commonwealth Declaration, Commonwealth Heads of Government pledged their countries to protect and promote the fundamental political values of the Commonwealth concentrating especially upon 'democracy, democratic processes and institutions which reflect national circumstances'. One of the most visible signs of this commitment is the development and work of human rights commissions (HRCs). Human rights commissions are established by the national constitution or by statute and are normally tasked with investigating allegations of human rights violations or discriminatory acts committed in violation of existing law by any person or body. Most also have a specific mandate to promote human rights.

The 1990s have seen a considerable increase in both their numbers and significance so that today HRCs operate in some 12 Commonwealth countries, both developing and developed, and these include some of the most influential and effective institutions in the world. Twin challenges still remain, that is, to encourage all Commonwealth countries to establish human rights commissions and to make such institutions as effective as possible. This is reflected in the Millbrook Commonwealth Action Programme which calls 'for assistance in creating and building the capacity of requisite institutions' as part of the measures in support of the Harare Principles.

Traditionally, there are several important differences between an office of the ombudsman and a human rights commission:

- HRCs are multi-member bodies whilst an office of the ombudsman is headed by a single individual;

- HRCs base their jurisdiction specifically on human rights norms whilst the prime concern for an ombudsman is the investigation of complaints from individual members of the public alleging 'maladministration' by public officials;

- an office of the ombudsman can only investigate complaints against public officials whilst the jurisdiction of HRCs normally extends to the private sector as well;

- unlike an office of the ombudsman, a HRC has a specific mandate to promote human rights;

2   The title of the institution varies from country to country but for the sake of convenience the term 'ombudsman' is used throughout this paper.

- HRCs undertake a variety of other human rights-related functions, such as reviewing proposed legislation for compliance with human rights;
- if a complaint is upheld, an ombudsman traditionally has no enforcement powers and is restricted to making recommendations to resolve the matter. HRCs enjoy wider enforcement powers, including in the case of the Uganda Human Rights Commission, the power to enforce its own decisions.

For the sake of convenience, we can loosely divide Commonwealth HRCs into the following categories:

HRCs based on domestic legislation

Most Commonwealth HRCs are tasked with the protection and promotion of human rights guaranteed under the Constitution. This, in itself, is a challenge especially given the fact that several Commonwealth countries have recently adopted new constitutions that protect a very wide range of human rights. Other commissions have more specialised functions. For example, the Canadian Human Rights Commission is responsible for ensuring that principles of equal opportunity and non-discrimination are implemented in all areas of federal jurisdiction.

HRCs based on international human rights instruments

Some commissions have a specific responsibility for encouraging and implementing international human rights standards. This is exemplified by the Australian Human Rights and Equal Opportunity Commission which administers legislation based directly on, or incorporating, United Nations human rights instruments.

Basing the work of a HRC on such instruments has several advantages. For example:

(a) they serve as a convenient point of reference by which the degree of domestic implementation of human rights may be assessed;

(b) the domestic procedure is far quicker and cheaper than resorting to the international machinery for the protection of human rights;

(c) gaps in domestic human rights legislation can be readily overcome by reliance on the relevant international human rights instrument.

A case in point is the United Kingdom which has incorporated the European Convention on Human Rights into domestic law (see the Human Rights Act 1998) so that, as from 2000, its provisions are enforceable by the courts.

However, there are many other international human rights conventions that are not enforceable in the United Kingdom in this way, for example, the United Nations Convention on the Rights of the Child. This could be overcome by allowing a human rights commission, the establishment of which remains tantalisingly elusive in the United Kingdom, to follow the Australian approach.

Overall, this model seems best able to provide for the systematic monitoring, enforcement and promotion of human rights.

'Quasi' human rights commissions

Today, some offices of the ombudsman also undertake responsibilities similar to those of a human rights commission. For example, in Namibia and Zimbabwe, the offices of the ombudsman may investigate complaints by individuals or groups alleging human rights violations by government officials and persons, enterprises and other private institutions as well as investigating complaints concerning maladministration by government officials. The incumbent also has a responsibility for promoting human rights.

From the practical point of view, this type of 'quasi' human rights commission may prove less effective than a full-blown human rights commission in that not only can the lack of a collegiate body have a negative impact on the independence of the institution itself, but it may also lead to an excessive work load for the existing staff.

THE ROLE OF PARLIAMENT IN SUPPORTING THE WORK OF NATIONAL INSTITUTIONS

The recognition in the Harare Commonwealth Declaration that democratic institutions must 'reflect national circumstances' means that there is no 'model' national institution. Thus the jurisdiction and powers of individual institutions will inevitably vary from State to State. Even so, there is one constant: every effective institution must be *demonstrably independent and enjoy adequate funding, staffing and resources*. Without these prerequisites, national institutions are a 'front and a facade' and a waste of scarce national resources in that they can give a totally false impression of a government's commitment to administrative justice and/or the protection and promotion of human rights.

In order to maintain these prerequisites, the support of parliament is necessary in a number of ways.

Parliamentary responsibility for appointments

One of the major reasons for the ineffectiveness of some national institutions is overt executive involvement in their organisation and operation.[3] From time to time a national institution may well be called upon to investigate sensitive areas of national life which government may wish to remain hidden. To operate effectively, it is absolutely essential that the institution is, and is perceived by the public as being, independent. This requires a procedure that allows for the appointment of persons who enjoy the confidence both of complainants and complainees that investigations will be undertaken impartially. It follows that overt executive involvement in the appointment process, and the appointment of those whose independence is questionable, is inappropriate. This point is neatly illustrated by the experience of the ombudsman in Swaziland where the incumbent was appointed by the executive. He also held the post of Secretary to the *Liqoqo* (Supreme Council of State), a position that was incompatible with his position as ombudsman. All this seriously tarnished the image of the office as an independent body in the eyes of the public and contributed greatly to the eventual failure of the office and its eventual dissolution.[4]

Somewhat surprisingly, despite the inherent dangers, in several Commonwealth countries the executive still bears the responsibility for nominating or recommending appointees to the head of state.[5] It is argued that, to retain public confidence in the independence of a national institution, the appointment process must provide for transparency and accountability. Herein lies the importance of the role of the legislature. The linking of a national institution with the legislature arguably removes it from overt executive influence and places on parliamentarians the task and responsibility of ensuring that appointees are demonstrably independent.

Parliamentary involvement with national institutions has a long history. Traditionally the office of the ombudsman was closely linked with the legislature and indeed in Sweden (where the modern office originated) and other Scandinavian countries the ombudsman is still elected by parliament itself. Some Commonwealth jurisdictions have broadly adopted this approach. Thus, during the parliamentary debate leading to the parliamentary Commission (Ombudsman) Act 1962 in New Zealand, it was repeatedly stressed that the ombudsman was to be an officer of parliament and that he/she must enjoy its confidence. Accordingly, although actually appointed

---

3   See, generally, *op cit*, Hatchard, fn 1, pp 50–71.

4   The office was established in 1983 but it was scrapped by the government in 1987: see, further, Ayee, J, 'The Ombudsman experience in the Kingdom of Swaziland: a comment' [1988] *Verfassung und Recht in Ubersee* 8, p14.

5   Eg, the head of government (Canadian Human Rights Commission); the Council of State (Ghanaian Commission on Human Rights and Administrative Justice); and the Ministry of Justice (New Zealand Human Rights Commission).

by the Governor General, such appointment is made on the recommendation of the legislative body. Similarly, in Barbados the Governor General is required to submit the proposed appointment to both Houses of parliament for approval whilst in Samoa the appointment is made on the recommendation of the Legislative Assembly. A link with the legislature is also retained in St Lucia and Jamaica, where the Ombudsman is appointed by the Governor General acting on the recommendation of the Prime Minister after consultation with the Leader of the Opposition, and with the appointment of commissioners to the Uganda Human Rights Commission and the South African Human Rights Commission. In the South African case, commissioners are nominated by a joint standing committee of the National Assembly proportionately composed of members of all the political parties represented in both the Assembly and the Senate. Once nominees have received the support of a majority of the members of the Assembly, the State President must then make the formal appointments.

One potential problem with placing responsibility for appointments on parliament is that some Commonwealth legislatures are so dominated by one political party that members may well simply follow the dictates of the executive as regards appointments. There are ways to minimise the problem. Firstly, to require a special parliamentary majority for all appointments. This was provided for in the 1993 South African Constitution where candidates for appointment to the South African Human Rights Commission were required to obtain the support of 75% of members of the National Assembly and the Senate.[6] In some cases, a rigid numerical formula may be inappropriate, especially where parliamentary opposition is especially weak. Thus, an alternative, and arguably better approach, is to make the appointment of the ombudsman and human rights commissioners an all-party matter requiring, for example, the support of the majority of the members of the ruling party together with a majority of the members of the main opposition party (or parties).

An alternative approach is to include representatives of civil society in the appointment process. This is the approach favoured by the United Nations *Principles relating to the status of national institutions*[7] which recommend that the appointment procedure (for multi-member institutions) involve the 'pluralistic representation of the social forces (of civilian society) involved in the protection and promotion of human rights ...' including representatives of non-governmental organisations, and universities as well as parliament.[8] A

---

6   For reasons that are not immediately apparent, the provision was omitted in the 1996 Constitution.

7   Adopted by the United Nations as an annex to General Assembly resolution 48/134 of 20 December 1993.

8   See the Paris Principles, 'Composition and guarantees of independence and pluralism', para 1.

practical illustration of this approach comes from Malawi. Here, the ombudsman is nominated by members of the public and appointed by the all-party parliamentary Public Appointments Committee[9] with the President having no formal role to play. South Africa also adopted this practice with regard to the appointment of the Public Protector[10] although this is not a constitutional obligation.

Overall, the appointment process is a confidence-building exercise for both government and civil society that a national institution will undertake investigations effectively and impartially. Parliamentarians can play a key role in this by taking responsibility for making the necessary appointments although the formal endorsement of an ombudsman/commissioners by the Head of State is perhaps important in some countries as a means of maintaining and enhancing the profile and status of the institution.

Parliamentary responsibility for providing adequate funding and resources

An effective national institution requires the provision of adequate funds and resources in order to carry out its responsibilities. In practice, the ineffectiveness of many Commonwealth national institutions (NIs) is directly attributable to the lack of adequate resources. A further difficulty in some cases is the lack of financial autonomy whereby funding to the NI is channelled through a government department that may be itself liable to investigation by the institution. This is a most unfortunate situation because it can inevitably give rise to a perception (however inaccurate) in the mind of complainants of possible bias on the part of the NI when investigating a complaint against that department. As the Commissioner for Human Rights and Administrative Justice in Ghana has stated:

> I wish to express my view once again that the independence of the Commission can be fully realised only if its budget is submitted direct to parliament for vetting and approval.[11]

Allocating parliament the task of working directly with NIs can alleviate these concerns. For example, in Uganda, the administrative expenses of the Uganda Human Rights Commission are charged to the Consolidated Revenue Fund and parliament is required by the Constitution to 'ensure that adequate resources and facilities are provided to the Commission to enable it to perform its functions effectively'.[12] In practice, parliament has proved extremely

---

9   The Public Appointments Committee is appointed by the National Assembly with proportionate representation from all parties represented in the National Assembly: Article 56(7) of the Constitution of Malawi.

10 The name given to the Office of the Ombudsman.

11 *CHRAJ Second Annual Report*, 1995, pp 2–3. In the Report, the Commissioner complains bitterly about the practice whereby the Ministry of Finance and Economic Planning can cut the Commission's budget after a lengthy and cumbersome process.

12 Section 13 of the UHRC Act 1997.

supportive of the Commission and has readily agreed to its funding requests.[13]

Making national institutions responsible to parliament

Whilst it is vital to maintain the independence of NIs, the issue of their accountability is scarcely addressed in Commonwealth jurisdictions. The independence of a NI does not include insulating it from a regular review (although not supervision) of its activities and this is another potential task for parliament.

At present, most national institutions are merely required to send a copy of their annual report to parliament. This is not sufficient. In particular, there is no time limit set for the furnishing of the document and NIs in several Commonwealth countries remain years behind in the submission of their reports. In addition, there is no obligation on parliament to debate the report and, in practice it appears that frequently the document is effectively ignored. This is all quite unsatisfactory.

National institutions should be under an obligation to submit their annual reports to the legislature within a certain time. The ombudsman or relevant commissioners should then be required to appear before the appropriate parliamentary committee to discuss its contents and the performance of their institution. In addition, and in recognition of the need to provide accountability to the wider community, parliament should establish a formal advisory committee also containing representatives of civil society and government, whose activities would include holding regular consultations with the NI on its activities and providing it with advice, support and encouragement.

Parliamentarians can also play a key role in the removal from office of an ombudsman or individual human rights commissioner. Given that in many ways their status is akin to that of judges, it is encouraging to note that Commonwealth jurisdictions provide for a formal procedure for their removal from office. By holding NIs responsible to parliament means that the removal of an ombudsman or commissioner becomes solely a matter for the legislature. This point was considered in South Africa where the drafters of the 1996 Constitution were specifically charged with safeguarding the 'independence and impartiality' of the Public Protector. The procedure adopted envisaged a finding by a committee of the National Assembly that grounds of misconduct, incapacity or incompetence existed and that this

---

13 Even so, financial autonomy does not mean financial adequacy and with Uganda operating a cash budget, the amount of money available for the Commission depends upon the actual income of the Treasury: thus, whilst, in the financial year 1997/98, the Commission had been voted Uganda Shs 5 billion, this was reduced by the Treasury to Uganda Shs 1.3 billion.

finding be adopted by a resolution of a majority of the members of the National Assembly. Thereafter, the Public Protector would be removed from office by the President. The Constitutional Court did not[14] consider that provision adequately safeguarded the independence and impartiality of the office-holder and thus the draft Constitution was amended to require a resolution by a two-thirds majority of the members of the National Assembly.[15]

Overall, perhaps the role of parliament vis à vis national institutions is encapsulated in Uganda where the legislature is tasked by the Constitution to protect the status and operation of the Uganda Human Rights Commission by overseeing the appointment of commissioners and by voting adequate funding to the Commission. Further, it is required to make laws to regulate and facilitate its performance.[16] This latter provision is particularly useful if viewed as placing an obligation on parliament to monitor the work and functioning of the Commission and to take appropriate action in order to strengthen and support it.

ADVISING AND PROVIDING INFORMATION TO PARLIAMENTARIANS

I do not think the calibre of members is very good; that is why parliament is meaningless ... I wonder if some MPs read newspapers and books or even discuss with friends before coming to parliament ... Some MPs are unwitty.

These words were reportedly spoken in 1992 at a seminar of senior public servants by Didymus Mutasa, a former Speaker of the House of Assembly in Zimbabwe and at that time a senior government Minister. For his pains, he was found guilty of contempt of parliament and severely reprimanded by the Speaker.[17] It is not intended here to comment on the issue of the calibre of MPs or whether or not they are 'unwitty' but implicit in Mutasa's statement is a recognition that MPs must be well informed and advised about national affairs so that they are equipped to perform their duties effectively. There are several mechanisms for MPs to acquire the necessary information and advice both within parliament and outside, for example, the parliamentary library, use of research assistants, and submissions and reports from non-governmental organisations. There is no doubt that NIs themselves can also

---

14 The court was required to certify that the 1996 Constitution complied with certain Constitutional Principles.

15 Curiously, the removal of members of the Human Rights Commission still requires the approval of a majority of the members of the National Assembly.

16 Article 58 of the Constitution of Uganda.

17 See *Mutasa v Makombe* [1997] 2 LRC 314.

make a unique and significant contribution by providing parliamentarians with accurate, authoritative and objective information and advice on issues involving proposed legislation and human rights.

There are several specific problem areas where there is seemingly an information vacuum which NIs can usefully address.

The implications of proposed legislation

The volume and complexity of Bills coming before parliament continues unabated throughout the Commonwealth. The implications of a particular Bill may not always be readily understood or apparent to members. To carry out their functions, parliamentarians must have the opportunity to make themselves fully informed about the implications of the proposed legislation. The point is well illustrated by reference to the Zimbabwean experience concerning a Bill to amend the Constitution. As the Constitution is the supreme law, any amendment to it is a serious matter and requires considerable debate both within and without parliament. In most Commonwealth countries constitutional amendments also require a special (normally two-thirds) majority of all the members of the legislature. Particular care is needed where the amendment is specifically designed to overturn or undermine a decision of the apex court concerning the interpretation of a fundamental rights provision.

In the case of Zimbabwe, the problem arose from a 1993 decision of the Supreme Court of Zimbabwe in the *Catholic Commission* case[18] that the dehumanizing factor of prolonged delay, viewed in conjunction with the harsh and degrading conditions in the condemned section of the holding prison, meant that executing four condemned prisoners would have constituted inhuman and degrading treatment contrary to section 15(1) of the Constitution of Zimbabwe. Accordingly, the court directed that the death sentences be replaced by sentences of life imprisonment. It also gave a series of directions on the procedure for dealing with condemned prisoners and suggested that petitions of mercy should be dealt with expeditiously by the executive, with three months being suggested as a possible time-frame. This landmark decision was later followed by the Judicial Committee of the Privy Council[19] and drew critical acclaim from commentators.[20] Even so, it met with a negative response from the government and within weeks the

---

18 *Catholic Commission for Justice and Peace in Zimbabwe v Attorney General* 1993 (4) SA 239. The decision of the full (five person) bench was given by Gubbay CJ.

19 *Pratt and Morgan v Attorney General for Jamaica* [1993] 4 All ER 769.

20 See, for example, Schabas, WA, 'Soering's "Legacy: the Human Rights Committee and the Judicial Committee of the Privy Council take a walk down death row"' (1994) 43 ICLQ 913. It is also worth noting that Zimbabwean government public criticism of the judgment ceased after the decision in *Pratt and Morgan*.

Constitution of Zimbabwe Amendment (No 13) Act 1993 was passed which retrospectively exempted the death penalty from the scope of section 15(1). Members of parliament overwhelmingly approved the Bill.

Whilst the Act was passed in accordance with the constitutional requirements, the process is worrying. In particular, it is questionable whether all members of parliament were able and/or prepared to undertake a critical, objective and informed view of the proposed constitutional change. Thus, in the parliamentary debate on the Bill, the few members of parliament who did speak seemingly did not understand the Supreme Court decision and believed that its effect was to abolish the death penalty itself. Indeed, just 26 of the 150 members made any contribution to the debate on the Second Reading with only one member actually managing to state and analyse the ruling accurately.[21]

It is not acceptable for members to simply rely on the explanation of the scope of proposed legislation by the relevant Minister responsible for introducing the Bill for he/she may fail (for whatever reason) to give members a full, frank and objective assessment of it. Again the debate on the 1993 Act in Zimbabwe is illuminating. Here members of parliament were informed by the Minister of Justice, Legal and Parliamentary Affairs during the Second Reading that the decision of the Supreme Court 'allowed the *de facto* abolition of the death sentence by the judiciary' and that the judgment 'was to the effect that from the day a person is sentenced to death by the High Court, three months should be the maximum. If three months pass before he is executed ... then there is a delay, which in the opinion of the Supreme Court, vitiates the execution'.[22] As noted above, that was certainly not the ruling of the Supreme Court.

As the editorial in a leading Zimbabwean legal periodical put it, it is the role and duty of parliamentarians not to allow:

> ... amendments to fundamental rights provisions in the Constitution to be rushed through parliament. The people should expect their parliamentarians to consider with great care the implications of any measures which will have the effect of diluting fundamental rights provisions. The people expect parliament to uphold fundamental rights and not to acquiesce in a process which weakens these rights.[23]

This example emphasises the danger of legislation being passed in circumstances where parliamentarians are seemingly not fully aware or

---

21 See the contribution of Mr S Malunga in Parliamentary Debates 22 September 1994. Seemingly, only five Members were not in favour of the Bill although their contributions on the matter were not always very clear. Thus, one member asserted that 'the proposal should be supported and we should remove [the] death sentence for the democratic development of our nation': Mr Nyashanu, Parliamentary Debates, 28 September 1994.

22 Parliamentary Debates, 22 and 28 September 1993.

23 See the Editorial entitled 'A regrettable amendment' in (1994) 6 Legal Forum 1, pp 1–2.

informed of its implications. It follows that MPs must have access to objective and independent information and advice. Human rights commissions, being independent, multi-member bodies with commissioners being drawn from a cross-section of society and from a variety of backgrounds, are ideally suited to provide such assistance.

How this is done will vary. In New Zealand, the Human Rights Commission has established a scheme to provide information and assistance to MPs (see below). A more formal scheme operates in South Africa where the Human Rights Commission is required to examine all Bills to assess whether they are in accordance with the Bill of Rights and, if not, to lobby and submit proposals to parliament.[24] Whatever the arrangement, it is important for parliamentarians to realise the immense assistance that they can obtain from national institutions.

Compliance by the state with its international human rights obligations

Most Commonwealth countries are now parties to the main international and relevant regional human rights instruments. One of the major obligations of state parties is to submit regular periodic reports on the measures taken by them to give effect to the rights contained in the instruments and on the progress made in the enjoyment of those rights. In practice, the reporting record of many Commonwealth countries is woeful.[25] Often, they are not submitted or are submitted very late.

Parliament bears the responsibility for overseeing these matters although how often this is done is not clear. Part of the problem is one of an information vacuum and it is here that national institutions can assist. A good example is that of the Uganda Human Rights Commission which is tasked by the Constitution of Uganda with 'monitoring government's compliance with international human rights treaty and convention obligations'.[26] It remains to be seen how the Commission views this function[27] but a broad interpretation of 'monitoring' will require government to report to the Commission on compliance with its international human rights obligations. Presumably, the Commission will then recommend remedial action and inform parliament

---

24 The Commission also monitors the implementation of socio-economic rights by requiring organs of state to submit information on measures taken to realise those rights and is thus in an excellent position to provide appropriate information to parliamentarians.

25 See 'Reporting under International Human Rights Instruments by African Countries' (1994) 38 Journal of African Law 61.

26 Article 52(1)(h) of the Constitution of Uganda.

27 The Commission has only been in operation since 1997.

accordingly. Parliamentarians will then be able to further pressure the government to comply with its treaty obligations.

Providing information on the national human rights scene

The 'We did not know what was going on' defence has been used by many in the face of accusations that government ministers and parliamentarians failed to speak out or take action to prevent abuses of human rights. For example, the gross human rights violations that occurred in Matabeleland, Zimbabwe, during the 1980s took place whilst parliament remained in session. Yet, there was little or no effort by parliamentarians to penetrate the government's veil of secrecy that was drawn over the activities of the security forces: this despite the many reports circulating from NGOs about the situation. As a recent Report on the atrocities pertinently asks:

> Why was it that these human rights violations could occur on our very doorstep without most of us knowing about it? Why is it that it has taken so long for victims to be heard?[28]

Certainly, some of the blame lies with parliament where MPs palpably failed to question Ministers about the activities of the security forces and meekly assented to every government 'request' for a renewal of the state of emergency under whose guise many of the atrocities were perpetrated.

The manner in which NIs can help alleviate this information vacuum is demonstrated by the South African Human Rights Commission. The Commission is required to submit an annual report to parliament on the state of human rights and freedoms in the country. This role is significant in that it provides parliament with an objective and reliable assessment of the human rights situation in the country and can help prevent the 'we did not know' syndrome. Currently, there is no statutory duty on parliament to debate such reports and this is an unfortunate oversight for there remains a danger that the report might otherwise have little impact. Here, wide media coverage of the report may persuade parliamentarians of the importance of debating it.

The 'partnership' approach of the New Zealand Human Rights Commission provides an excellent model for the development of the relationship between parliamentarians and national institutions. In the Foreword to a detailed folder entitled *Information on Human Rights for Members of Parliament* and given to every individual MP, the Chief Commissioner states:

> Yours is the responsibility to provide a legislative environment, both domestically and internationally, in which all people present in New Zealand,

---

28   Catholic Commission for Justice and Peace in Zimbabwe/Legal Resources Foundation, *Breaking the Silence: Building True Peace – A Report on the Disturbances in Matabeleland and the Midlands 1980–88*, 1997, p 213.

both the privileged and marginalised, can reach their full potential to the benefit of us all.

Commissioners and staff of the Human Rights Commission are your partners in this task. Information and assistance is freely available to you. Together, we have a responsibility to protect and promote the human rights of the people of Aotearoa/New Zealand.

The Commission is committed to keeping MPs as well briefed as possible on human rights issues. To this end, we will provide you with topical updates to this folder, occasional papers based on work done by and for the Commission and bring you up to date with other news as appropriate.

The development of this 'partnership' approach is still in its infancy and only operates at any formal level in a handful of countries and even where it has been established its impact is not yet clear. Even so, it is a partnership that is worth pursuing and developing.

OVERVIEW

Developing a working partnership between national institutions and parliamentarians can make a significant contribution towards implementing the Harare Commonwealth Declaration. This calls for several things:

(1) There is a need to establish national institutions in all Commonwealth countries and parliamentarians should actively encourage their governments to do so. In doing so, they will be echoing the call in the Millbrook Commonwealth Action Programme 'for assistance in creating and building the capacity of requisite institutions' as part of the measures in support of the Harare Principles.

(2) In order to create and retain effective national institutions, parliament should have the responsibility of:

(a) supporting their work by maintaining the independence of the institutions and ensuring they enjoy adequate funding and staffing; and

(b) overseeing their work through, for example, debating the annual reports of NIs and by establishing a special parliamentary committee on national institutio •s.

(3) Whilst parliamentarians can obtain information and advice from a number of sources, national institutions are ideally suited to provide expert, independent and objective advice to them especially on issues relating to proposed legislation and human rights. Parliamentarians should seek to develop a close working relationship with national institutions to ensure that the fullest possible information is available to them to assist in their work.

CHAPTER 13

JUDICIAL REVIEW OF EXECUTIVE ACTION: GOVERNMENT UNDER THE LAW

RMA Chongwe

INTRODUCTION

In many Commonwealth states, checks and balances on the use of power are constantly being reinvented. Since I left law school some 30 years ago governments have created a huge variety of statutory watchdogs to keep an eye on the operations of both the public and private sector.

The first of these bodies in the part of the Commonwealth where I come from was the office of the ombudsman, formed in 1973 to deal with lots of smallish problems affecting people working in the civil service and in the public sector. It was felt at the time that this was very important, as it would underpin the right of public sector employees to complain against the bureaucratic decisions that adversely affected them.

In the Commonwealth of Australia, the Australian citizen's right to know the reasons for official decisions affecting their interests was enshrined in the Commonwealth Administrative Decisions (Judicial Review) Act 1977 which also created an Administrative Appeals Tribunal to review such decisions. Other watchdogs like the Permanent Human Rights Commission have been created recently in Zambia to monitor the enforcement of human rights and human rights legislation.

In the 1980s, there was a flurry of watchdog activity in response to the perceived crisis of official corruption. The Zambian government created the Anti-Corruption Commission in 1980 as an answer to the growing suspicion of the emergence of corruption in the growing public sector created as a result of the policy of nationalisation of privately owned enterprises. The morality of the sector and the civil service had to be kept in check and watched. Later in 1987, the watchdog on narcotic drugs had to be created in the wake of the growing incidents in drug dealing and drug trafficking.

One of the main reasons that watchdogs have gone forth and multiplied is that traditional legal processes have become cumbersome and inaccessible to ordinary people. However, these watchdogs can only properly function in an atmosphere of independence and impartiality, accessibility, efficiency and effectiveness, openness and accountability. To safeguard the independence of these schemes, those appointed to handle complaints need greater employment security than they have at present. Moves towards greater accountability often encounter resistance from the bureaucratic culture.

Statutory watchdogs are appointed by governments to make governments accountable, and therein lies their fatal flaw: nobody wants the doberman at their own back door. Watchdogs who are merely left to watch and are never allowed to bite tend to lose enthusiasm over time. As they become familiar with those they are watching, they find that it is easier to be 'reasonable', to accommodate and co-operate, than to engage in constant confrontation. Friendly watchdogs may live to a comfortable old age, but public confidence in them tends to suffer.

In the case of those that are created in the developing part of the Commonwealth and are as a result of appeasing donor-funding requirements, they may exist merely as a source for obtaining donor aid, which is in very high demand. Their creation may have nothing to do with the improvement in the delivery of services to the people. In Zambia, the Anti-Corruption Commission, the Drug Enforcement Commission, and the Permanent Human Rights Commission have been correctly labelled (in my opinion) by some, as agencies of illusion, not reality, deliberately set up by the executive in such a way as to give the appearance of doing something, but deliberately given neither the resources nor authority to do anything. The record of these commissions in Zambia is far from being impressive, and their respective tiny budgets are a joke. The Anti-Corruption Commission and the Drug Enforcement Commission are, as organisations, almost completely ineffective and a total waste of time.

A representative democracy has to protect individual rights, but there are tensions between these rights and the organisational needs of government. Until there is some internalisation of these principles by those who rule us, watchdogs will continue to be essential, and they will also continue to be threatened, diminished and abolished, especially if they do their jobs well. There is no certain way of protecting watchdogs against a hostile government, but it is possible to pre-empt some of the problems that emerge when government tires of having them around.

As a matter of government policy, watchdogs need to have an assured distance from other government policies. This means that office-holders must have: secure tenure; a clear mandate; an explicit set of values; and must be accountable to the people's representatives in parliament, not to the executive. They are unlikely to retain their independence if they are subject to the discretionary power of those they are set up to watch. For the watchdogs themselves there is a delicate balance to be struck. There is a difference between retaining the integrity of the office and acting in a high-handed way.

THE JUDICIARY AND THE EXECUTIVE

There is a clear distinction which has to be drawn between the law-makers and those who assist in interpreting it and the actual interpreters. A distinguished French jurist warned many years ago about the tyranny which would befall a state where there was no division of governmental authority and instead the authority was fused in one body. In his book, *The Spirit of the Law*, Montesquieu wrote in the 18th century:

> There is no liberty if the judiciary power be not separated from the legislature and the executive. Were it joined with the legislative, the life and liberty of the subject would be exposed to arbitrary control; for the judge would then be the legislator. Were it joined to the executive power, the judge might behave with violence and oppression.

Indeed, it is this principle that led the founders of the United States Constitution to institute a near separation of powers: the law-making power in the Congress; the executive in the President; and the judicial in the Supreme Court. This occurred in very few of the member states of the Commonwealth of Nations. Even in the member states which became republics after their attainment of independence, the separation of the powers set out in their various constitutions has rarely followed that of the United States. This is because in most Commonwealth countries there does still exist responsible government where ministers of the state: are directly accountable to the representatives of the people in parliament; are themselves members of the parliament; are drawn from the elected or nominated members of parliament; and are expected to sit in parliament and be prepared to answer questions from the members concerning their ministry. There are no substitutes for the ministers in parliament as is the practice in continental Europe.

Judicial independence is cardinal to the sustenance of a democratic culture and the democratic process because without it there is nothing else to check and control the chaos and anarchy that may befall a State and its people. It is for this reason that judicial independence is the subject of various international treaties to which most member states of the United Nations Organisation are party, including my own country, Zambia.

Article 10 of the Universal Declaration of Human Rights provides that 'all people are entitled to a fair public hearing by an independent tribunal'. Article 14.1 of the International Covenant on Civil and Political Rights states that 'Everyone shall be entitled to a fair hearing by a competent, independent and impartial tribunal established by law'. Under the Basic Principles on the Independence of the Judiciary endorsed by the United Nations in 1985, judges 'must have tenure, and be free from direct or indirect pressure in the performance of their duties'. These principles reinforce the point that governments may not abolish courts and judicial positions in order to get rid of an inconvenient judge. Otherwise as Michael Kirby, a judge of the Australian High Court, has said:

> ... the threat hangs as a Damoclean sword over all judicial officers in a like position. If judicial officers are repeatedly removed from their offices and afforded equivalent or higher appointments, the inference must be drawn that their tenure is, effectively, at the will of the executive government.[1]

He added:

> A decision-maker who must examine and weigh up evidence and submissions fairly and reach conclusions affecting powerful and opinionated interests, must be put beyond the risk of retaliation and retribution. That is what the tenure of judges and other independent office-holders is about. It concerns giving substance to the promise that important decisions will be made neutrally: without fear or favour, affection or ill will.

Judges of the common law have always had power to supervise the jurisdiction of tribunals appointed to perform quasi-judicial matters through the power of review. This power was exercised in circumstances where the tribunal was guilty of the following: excess of the jurisdiction conferred on it; absence of the jurisdiction; failure to exercise the jurisdiction; failure to observe rules of natural justice; and denial of a hearing to one of the parties to the dispute.

In those circumstances, prerogative writs would be issued against the inferior tribunal to force it to do what it should have done under the rules establishing its jurisdiction. The injunction was later to be very widely used to restrain a public corporation or officer from taking a decision, which it was argued, would adversely affect the rights of the party applying for the order.

JUDICIAL REVIEW OF EXECUTIVE ACTION

Judicial review is a very powerful weapon in the armoury of the courts to review a decision that has been made by a member of the executive or an administrator which it is alleged: was made improperly; without authority or in excess of the powers conferred on the decision-maker; or because of the failure by the decision-maker to observe the rules of natural justice.

In ordinary parlance people loosely say that they have applied to the court for judicial review or they are asking for review. All this means the same thing and is merely a different way of expressing it. The power of administrators and that of the politicians to make decisions affecting the lives of the people has grown over the years. As a result it has therefore become necessary for this power to be checked.

---

1   Kirby, M, 'The Abolition of Courts and Non-Reappointment of Judicial Officers in Australia', Ronald Wilson Lecture, Perth, 28 November 1994.

At the turn of the last century, Dicey, writing about the British Constitution, wrote dismissively about administrative law, which had developed in France and continental Europe. He said that English law did not acknowledge the existence of such a thing as administrative law as was being practised by French civil servants. Before the end of this century, however, what was said by Dicey as not being part of the common law, is in fact part of our law. As I mentioned at the beginning of this paper, some Commonwealth governments have had in place courts to deal with administrative matters. A decision of a municipal council refusing to allow young people to enter their theatre to watch a film on a Sunday has been held 'unreasonable' (*Associated Provincial Picture Houses v Wednesbury Corporation*).[2] A decision refusing members of the British secret service from joining a trade union has been held reasonable (*Council of Civil Service Unions v Minister for the Civil Service*).[3]

The executive in England has not seen it as usurpation of its powers in appointing a judge of the High Court (Scott J) to investigate members of the executive for their role in the wake of persistent allegations that a law banning the sale and supply of arms to Iraq may have been breached on instructions by some members of the executive.

Judicial review as a legal remedy has proved very popular in England and in some parts of the Commonwealth. It is less formalised and therefore less cumbersome, it is expeditious and cheaper and only requires the applicant to satisfy the following criteria: the proceedings must be commenced within six months of the making of the decision; leave of the court must be obtained before making the application; and the application must be made to a High Court judge. The decision-maker may have been a government minister or a top civil servant or a committee of the executive or a commission set up by the executive. It is sufficient if the applicant can prove that the decision-maker was motivated by malice in coming to his/her decision, or that such person exceeded their powers provided for by the statute or that the rules of natural justice were not followed.

On the African continent, the growth of judicial review has been largely linked to preventive detention cases. Detention of citizens is either provided for under security regulations or pursuant to a declaration of a state of emergency. The decision to detain is largely made by the head of the executive of the country concerned. Even if an official is empowered to sign the actual detention order, it is usually on the instructions of a member of the executive. The detention can usually be challenged through the application for a writ of *habeas corpus*. Since the introduction of the process of judicial review as set out in the White Book under Order 57, Zambians have taken advantage of the procedure and challenges to detention orders have been made through application to the court for judicial review.

---

2   [1948] 1 KB 223.

3   [1985] AC 374.

Since 1992, the Legal and Constitutional Affairs Division of the Commonwealth Secretariat has been conducting seminars in developing Commonwealth states on the judicial review of decisions made by the executive and top government administrators. To these seminars and workshops have come politicians, judges, magistrates, senior civil servants, the police and lawyers both in government service and in private practice. The seminars have been very useful and almost all the senior civil servants who have attended the courses have been in a position to express how grateful and helpful they have been.

These seminars have had to deal with the role of administrators as decision-makers and the necessity for them to communicate directly with the officer in respect of whom a decision has been made. If a complaint has been made against an officer, that officer should be given an opportunity to be heard and this should be in the presence of his/her accusers who should also repeat the accusations in the officer's presence. In the case of Zambia, the country witnessed unprecedented growth of administrative law before the current government came into office. This development was gradual. It was not unusual for a person who had been detained by the executive to be released by the court, only to be re-arrested and re-detained soon after. With the growth in maturity of the members of the executive, the decisions of the court came to be respected. The court on its part started to go behind the detention warrant to ascertain the reasons for the detention. It was no longer sufficient for the State merely to prove that the detention warrant was signed by the President and that therefore the court could not go beyond the warrant. It was no longer sure that the court would not investigate whether a prima facie case did exist on which such a presidential decision could have been made. Where there was no such prima facie case, the court did not hesitate to invalidate the detention and set the detainee free. The Law Association of Zambia was in a position in 1995 to sponsor a book *Civil Liberties Cases in Zambia* (Ndulo, M and Turner, K (eds)) which traced this development.

The situation has since changed. The last state of emergency was proclaimed on 29 October 1997 and lifted on 17 March 1998. During this time, applications for writs of *habeas corpus* were rendered irrelevant as the courts refused to grant the writs once they had merely sighted the detention warrant and the signature of the President on it!

An application to a High Court judge for leave for the judicial review of a decision of the Zambian Citizenship Board made in 1964 granting Zambian citizenship to the former President, Kenneth Kaunda, was granted by the judge sitting at *nisi prius*. Kaunda appealed to the Supreme Court of Zambia on the ground that the court had no jurisdiction to grant judicial review of an administrative decision, which was made 34 years before. The Supreme Court of Zambia presided over by the Deputy Chief Justice dismissed the appeal on the ground that the question raised was one of public interest that should not be glossed over by legal technicalities.[4]

The Supreme Court of Zambia is the highest court in the land. The higher courts in Zambia derive their jurisdiction in cases of judicial review from the provisions of Order 57 of the White Book in use in England and Wales. The High Court of Zambia has not made its own rules to regulate the court's practice and procedure in matters of judicial review. It is such behaviour by the courts that has the effect of eroding the confidence of the people in their judiciary.

In other parts of Africa, judicial review has taken root and in the case of Malawi, Namibia, South Africa and Seychelles, this is incorporated in their various constitutional documents. There is, however, need for seminars and workshops aimed at training African administrators in the field of administration. The cost for conducting these seminars is horrendous, particularly for a good number of the countries in the developing Commonwealth. They can ill afford to meet the costs of these seminars that are essential for the development of administrative law and good administration. Taking into account the stated desire of some developed nations to provide aid to the Third World, perhaps this is an area where the donor community would be interested in assisting. Such assistance has the beneficial effect of helping to build civil service capacity on the African continent, which is very much in short supply.

CONCLUSION

The development of administrative law can provide ordinary people with the hope that should an axe fall on them unfairly as they go about their daily life there can be a remedy which is easily available to them. It is important for people to know they will be in a position to receive natural justice should the need arise. The rise of bureaucracy over the past 50 years has been formidable and while this creates a large degree of security for societies, it also creates institutions, both private and public which can also be so massive as to dwarf the ordinary person.

It is important that we have, in all Commonwealth jurisdictions, judges who have the backbone to review decisions of the highest officers in the land and to pass judgment on these without fear and favour. To be effective in this area the highest standards of professionalism are required from our judiciary.

---

4   *Remmy Mushota and Patrick Katyoka v Kenneth David Kaunda*, Supreme Court of Zambia, 1997 (unreported).

CHAPTER 14

JUDGES AND PARLIAMENTARIANS: THE PUBLIC PERCEPTION

Colin Nicholls QC

INTRODUCTION

In 1983 and 1993, two MORI public opinion polls conducted in England offered respondents a list of people in different occupations and asked of each 'Would you tell me whether you generally trust them to tell the truth or not?'. The 1983 results disclosed that only 16% and 18% of respondents trusted government ministers and politicians respectively to tell the truth. By 1993 the figures had declined to 11% and 14%. The polls asked the same question about judges. They fared much better, but not as well as priests. They scored 77%. However, by 1993, this figure had declined to 68%.[1] The question was not asked about lawyers.

Public anxiety following a spate of allegations in England and a suggestion of 'sleaze' in the late 1990s led to the Conservative government setting up in 1994 the Committee on Standards in Public Life under Lord Nolan. In its first report published in May 1995, it confirmed that the anxiety was 'widely shared and deeply felt', but concluded that much of it was based on perceptions and beliefs not supported by facts. The concern had increased, but it was impossible to say that standards had declined. It could be that expectations had increased.

The Committee's inquiry confirmed, as Lord Steyn observed in his lecture to the Administrative Law Association in 1996, that 'rightly the public view the conduct of all arms of government – and the judiciary is one – with intense scepticism' and that 'a sceptical and ever watchful public opinion is the best guarantee of the democratic process'.[2]

NEW LABOUR

Lord Nolan's committee warned that, unless corrective measures were taken promptly, there was a danger that anxiety and suspicion would give way to

---

1   *Standards in Public Life*, First Report of the Committee on Standards in Public Life, Chairman Lord Nolan, Cm 2850-1, Volume 1 Report, Appendix 1, pp 104–08.

2   *The Weakest and Least Dangerous Department of Government*, 1996 Administrative Law Association lecture, delivered at Lincoln's Inn on 27 November 1996.

disillusion and growing cynicism. Since then, the committee has published two further reports and covered all aspects of English public life.

The new Labour government was elected to office committed to a programme of constitutional and legal reform. It re-declared war on corruption and sleaze in order, in the words of the Home Secretary, not just to 'to restore public confidence' but 'to set an example elsewhere'. The law of bribery is being re-defined including the bribery of MPs, a statutory offence of misuse of public office is being created and there is to be stronger self-regulation by parliament under a parliamentary Commissioner for Standards. The United Kingdom has signed the European Union Convention on Corruption and the Organisation of Economic Co-operation and Development (OECD) treaty criminalising bribery of foreign public officials in international business transactions. Within the Commonwealth the Report of the Expert Group on Good Governance and Elimination of Corruption in Economic Management will be submitted to the Commonwealth Heads of Government at their next meeting. That report will embrace issues of public sector remuneration, ethical standards in the private sector, and the educational processes needed to encourage an anti-corruption culture in society.

Also in the new government's law reform programme is the incorporation of the European Convention of Human Rights (ECHR). The United Kingdom which prides itself on its unwritten constitution is to have a written Bill of Rights. The incorporation of the ECHR is effected by the Human Rights Act 1998. It incorporates the Convention and its case law into English law so that English judges will be required to apply the law of the ECHR as well as English law.

Judges will be required to interpret statutes in conformity with the ECHR and develop the common law with regard to the terms of the Convention. As the Lord Chancellor said of its interpretation in his Tom Sargent Memorial Lecture 1997:

> The courts' decisions will be based on a more overtly principled, indeed moral basis. The court will look at the positive right. It will only accept an interference with that right where a justification, allowed under the Convention, is made out. The scrutiny will not be limited to seeing if the words of an exception can be satisfied. The court will need to be satisfied that the spirit of this exception is made out. It will need to be satisfied that the spirit of this interference with the protected right is justified in the public interest in a free democratic society. Moreover, the courts in this area will have to apply the Convention principle of proportionality. This means that the court will be looking substantively at that question. It will not be limited to a secondary view of the decision-making process but at the primary question of the merits of the decision itself.[3]

---

3   'The development of human rights in Britain under an incorporated Convention on Human Rights' [1998] PL 223.

Judges will also have power to declare primary legislation incompatible with the ECHR. There will then be a 'fast track' procedure to ensure amendment of the relevant legislation. It will be unlawful for public authorities to act in a way incompatible with the ECHR and the courts will be able to provide a remedy for any violation. The power of the English courts to 'declare' legislation incompatible, as opposed to their being able to strike it down, is consistent with the limited power of the ECHR itself, which is merely to declare the existence of a violation. The limitation on the power of the courts in this respect appears to preserve the sovereignty of parliament. However, the tenor of the Lord Chancellor's remarks in his keynote address to this Colloquium was that legislation would be dutifully amended. In this respect, it is significant that the United Kingdom has loyally remedied the numerous violations declared by the ECHR since it submitted to its jurisdiction.

Rodger Chongwe said during the course of discussion in this Colloquium that the constitution, not the supremacy of parliament, is the yardstick for African countries. In a Commonwealth – indeed a world – where the threat of tyranny is a constant reality and where fundamental freedoms are universal and enduring truths, it is difficult to justify the United Kingdom's ambivalent attitude to their supremacy. Even more so when the United Kingdom has for a long time submitted to the power to strike down its laws when they are repugnant to the rules of the European Union.

CORRUPTION WORLDWIDE

Although as can be judged from events since 1993, English politicians had no reason to congratulate themselves on the results of the MORI poll on the integrity of politicians and judges, it is alarming to consider what the responses might have been if the questions had been asked or permitted to be asked in other countries of the developed and developing world, including countries in the Commonwealth.

The rule of law depends on the integrity of government and the ability of judges to ensure government keeps within the law and respects fundamental freedoms. If the public perception of politicians is that the conferment of public office is regarded as a licence for corruption and that the judges are powerless to prevent it, the rule of law itself is threatened. As Heather Hallet, QC, Chairman of the General Council of the Bar for England and Wales, said at the Annual Bar Conference on 12 June 1998, a government committed to law and order should remember that the rule of law will survive only as long as the public has confidence in it and, as Dame Silvia Cartwright said at this Colloquium: '... without the respect of the community the judiciary cannot survive.'

In severely deprived parts of the world the people's perception of the integrity of politicians might seem to be irrelevant. As Mr Akufo Addo, MP, said, of Ghana '40 years after independence most of my people are illiterate'. All the world's deprived people want is government that gives them freedom from war, disease and poverty and the same for their children. For those who comprehend the democratic process, that need is for governments which are freely elected and which keep their promises. Also, for access to independent courts which settle their disputes impartially and speedily, provide adequate remedies and guarantee fundamental rights. It is to their perceptions that today's question is directed.

GUIDELINES

The Nolan Report and other polls[4] conducted in the 1990s disclosed that, in England, there was confusion as to what was acceptable behaviour in society generally, and particularly within government. So far as the world generally is concerned, there is a culture of corruption endowed by custom with an acceptability no longer to be tolerated. It is not surprising that Lord Nolan concluded that:

(1) the seven general principles – selflessness, integrity, objectivity, accountability, openness, honesty and leadership – need to be re-stated;

(2) codes of conduct need to be drawn up;

(3) systems need to be devised for monitoring them; and

(4) more should be done to promote and reinforce standards of conduct in public bodies, particularly through guidance and training.

The objective of this colloquium is to assist in the drafting of codes/guidelines of good practice on parliamentary sovereignty and the independence of the judiciary. The title of this 6th Session, 'Judges, Parliamentarians and Civil Society', for the first time introduces 'Civil Society', by which I understand 'the people', into the equation.

Just as we have striven in previous sessions to draft codes on the independence of the judiciary and its relationship with parliament, so also we need to draft codes of acceptable behaviour and codes which include educating the people as to how those codes will be observed by judges and parliamentarians. Only in that way can they have a true perception of the integrity of government. As Mr Justice Dowd said at this colloquium: 'Politicians and judges need guidelines on ethics'. The public must be educated on the rules which govern their parliaments and judges. Codes of

---

4   Gallup Poll, 1985 and 1994, and Gallup survey 1997.

practice must be drawn up to improve the public's perception and the public must know that offenders will be accountable for breaches of rules and disqualified from their respective offices.

CHAPTER 15

FREE SPEECH: PARLIAMENTARY PRIVILEGE AND THE SUB JUDICE RULE

Rt Hon Paul East, QC, MP

John Stewart Mill well understood the importance of the free press as an effective control of government when he said:

> So true it is, however, that the discontent of the people is the only means of removing the defects of vicious governments, that the freedom of the press, the main instrument of creating discontent, is in all civilised countries, among all but the advocates of misgovernment, regarded as an indispensable security, and the greatest safeguard of the interests of mankind.

But, a free press is only as good as the information it receives. That is why freedom of information legislation is so important. New Zealand passed such a law in 1982. The government in the United Kingdom is currently considering such legislation.

The law passed in New Zealand effectively reverses the normal government practice. All information is made public unless there is good reason for it to remain secret rather than the reverse. The Official Information Act 1982 sets out the circumstances in which information may remain secret. In broad terms, such information is not released if it is likely to prejudice the security, defence or economic well being of New Zealand. Other grounds for refusing the release of information include the need to maintain free and frank debate and discussion for the effective conduct of public affairs.

If a government minister makes a decision to keep information secret then the person applying for the information may challenge that decision. At the time our law was passed, there was considerable political debate on this point. In particular, the view was expressed that the courts should not be involved in ruling on this decision. Eventually, all political parties in parliament agreed that rather than lead the courts into an area of litigation likely to be highly political, it was better to use the office of the ombudsman. If a minister refuses to release information, the person applying for the information has a right of appeal to the ombudsman. If the ombudsman rules in favour of the applicant, then the information must be released unless the government is prepared to make an Order in Council – effectively overruling the ombudsman. The making of an Order in Council involves the whole Cabinet, in the full light of public scrutiny, and may be subject to examination by a parliamentary select committee – the Regulations Review Select Committee. The committee has been established to provide parliamentary scrutiny of regulations.

The Regulations Review Select Committee has been a particularly useful innovation. So much legislation today is now passed by regulation rather than Act of parliament. This is often a necessary measure for the effective management of government. However, such legislation often faces little public scrutiny. In New Zealand a parliamentary committee now takes this task. By convention, this committee is chaired by an opposition member of parliament and is empowered by our standing orders to examine any regulation put forward by the executive and to report to parliament on the regulation.

There is some uncertainty as to whether an Order in Council is a regulation as defined in New Zealand statute law and therefore able to be examined by the Regulations Review Select Committee. While there has been no definitive interpretation of this issue, it may be that in New Zealand we will move to ensure that Orders in Council are treated in the same way as other regulations and there is no doubt that the parliamentary select committee may examine them.

Any Order in Council resulting from an official information request must set out the reasons for which it is made and the grounds supporting those reasons. Application may be made to the High Court challenging the making of an Order in Council but only on these procedural grounds.

FREEDOM OF THE PRESS

Is it necessary to have statutory recognition to ensure freedom of the press? Whilst the need will probably vary from country to country, it is certainly likely to be required in some jurisdictions. In New Zealand for many years, press freedom was reliant on the common law. The passage of the New Zealand Bill of Rights Act 1990 saw for the first time statutory protection for the press. Section 14 reads:

> Freedom of expression – Everyone has the right to freedom of expression, including the freedom to seek, receive, and impart information and opinions of any kind in any form.

While the New Zealand Bill of Rights Act is not entrenched and is unable to strike down other laws passed by parliament, this legislation has certainly been relied on by the courts to uphold press freedom.

PARLIAMENTARY PRIVILEGE AND SUB JUDICE RULE

In a way, these are linked in that both are reflections of the long-standing relationship between the Houses of parliament and the courts of law. In New

Zealand, this is best described as 'the doctrine of mutual restraint'. It is a relationship that is of the highest constitutional significance. It is one that should be marked by mutual respect and restraint. On the one hand, the law requires the courts not to question the proceedings of parliament. On the other, our parliament and many others have adopted rules aimed at maintaining respect for the judiciary and avoiding the creation of prejudice to any pending court proceedings. New Zealand members of parliament may not make unbecoming references to judges, although this does not prohibit debate or criticism of the court structure or, indeed, of a judicial decision.

The sub judice rule is set out in the standing orders of the New Zealand House of Representatives. They contain a prohibition on the reference to and debate of any matter that is awaiting trial by the court if the Speaker believes there is a real danger of prejudice to the case in question. The enforcement of the rule is at the discretion of the chair and indeed the House expressly reserves the right to debate a particular court case if it is the subject of legislation. So, the House does not retreat from its right to amend the law as a result of litigation before the courts and to allow debate on particular court cases if such legislation is before the House.

PARLIAMENTARY PRIVILEGE AND THE PRESS

One of the leading cases on this subject is *Donohoe v Canadian Broadcasting Corporation*.[1] In that case, the Supreme Court of Canada in a well reasoned decision overturned the Appeal Division and upheld parliament's right through its inherent privileges to exclude television cameras from the debating chamber. This was despite the fact that these parliamentary privileges are mentioned only in passing in the Preamble to the Canadian Constitution Act 1867. The Act proclaimed an intention to establish a 'constitution similar in principle to that of the United Kingdom'. In New Zealand, section 242 of the Legislature Act 1980 provides the New Zealand parliament with the same rights and privileges as are enjoyed by the House of Commons in the United Kingdom. It is therefore quite clearly spelled out that such inherent privileges are incorporated into the domestic law of New Zealand.

In any event, the most important parliamentary privilege, that of freedom of speech, is probably already incorporated in the domestic laws of most Commonwealth countries. That is because it flows from Article 9 of the Bill of Rights 1688:

---

1   [1993] 1 SCR 319.

> That the Freedome of Speech and Debates or Proceedings in Parlyement ought not to be impeached or questioned in any court or place out of Parlyement.

The principle behind Article 9 is as relevant now as it was in 1688. Its rationale was spelled out in the 1994 Privy Council decision in *Prebble v Television New Zealand*.[2] It expresses:

> The need to ensure so far as possible that a member of the legislature and witnesses before the House can speak freely without fear that what they say will later be held against them in the courts.

It is in the public interest that members and witnesses are not inhibited in any way from speaking fully and freely. It is not a privilege that exists for the benefit of members but for the benefit of the parliamentary system. In *Prebble*, affidavits filed in the court in those proceedings referred to speeches made by members of parliament in the House of Representatives for the purposes of impugning the motives of the members in making these speeches. The High Court upheld the argument advanced by the House of Representatives that such evidence should be struck out. The Court of Appeal agreed that the evidence should be struck out but stayed the action on the basis that it was unfair to proceed without the material from parliament. The Privy Council resolutely and clearly confirmed the protection offered by Article 9 and held that the action could proceed without it.

It was never argued that Article 9 should be interpreted literally and that questioning actions in parliament in some other place such as a newspaper was outlawed. It applies when the maker of the statement could be placed in jeopardy by court action.

To further complicate the issue, there are exemptions. An example being the use of Hansard (the record of parliamentary debate) as an aid to statutory interpretation. This was confirmed for the United Kingdom by the decision of the House of Lords in *Pepper v Hart*.[3] It has already become established practice in New Zealand. It is also permissible to give evidence in court that certain events happened in parliament: such as the fact that a speech was made, or a Bill was passed, or that members voted in a certain way. That is allowed because there is no risk of impeaching or questioning what happened in parliament merely by giving factual evidence of what occurred in the House. But, the court must go no further – it is for parliament to conduct and judge its own affairs not the courts and members must be protected from court action for anything they say in parliament.

To draw from this article certain suggestions which may be of use to other Commonwealth countries, it is fair to claim that New Zealand is well satisfied with:

---

2   [1994] 3 WLR 970.
3   [1993] AC 593.

(1) Freedom of information legislation which requires all information to be made public unless there is good reason for secrecy. A right of appeal exists to the ombudsman and this decision can only be overturned by an Order in Council.

(2) Regulations passed by the government are subject to scrutiny by a parliamentary select committee – the Regulations Review Select Committee which is chaired by an opposition member of parliament and reports directly to parliament.

(3) The standing orders of the New Zealand House of Representatives require respect for the judiciary and set out the sub judice rule.

(4) The inherent privileges of parliament are incorporated into domestic law so that there is no doubt about their application.

CHAPTER 16

JUDGES AND PARLIAMENTARIANS:
THE PUBLIC PERCEPTION

Justice Rasheed A Razvi

At the very outset, please allow me to say that the public perception in Pakistan about the judges and parliamentarians is quite different from the experience of Western countries. This is so since there is an essential difference in the growth of parliamentary democracy in the West and in a neo-colonial society like Pakistan. In the West, parliamentary democracy emerged after the death of feudalism and the emergence of a new socio-economic order born out of the Industrial Revolution. In countries like ours, the old socio-economic order was prevailing when the Indo-Pakistan subcontinent was colonised by the British. These colonial masters enforced their own structure of the state and the institutions which were not linked with the economic base of the society. This is what has been described by one historian as an over-developed state structure in neo-colonial societies.

Resultantly, parliamentary institutions were created but those entering them did not necessarily fully represent public opinion. Most of the elected members entered parliament not because their views were popular but because they came from influential land-owning families and enjoyed semi-feudal powers in the rural areas. These people hardly considered themselves accountable to their poor and illiterate electorates for their performance. Thus, a class of people were born and bred during the years of British Raj in the Indo-Pakistan subcontinent.

With the growth of society, an enlightened middle class started emerging, particularly in urban areas. After 1947, when Pakistan became an independent state, the growth of the middle classes continued which, to some extent, got its strength from the migration of millions of people from India into the urban areas of Pakistan. But this small middle class found very little representation in institutions such as parliament. The landed aristocracy continued to have control over representative institutions. Its interests were opposed to those of the new emerging small business and middle classes and the common people. This aristocracy had enjoyed a great deal of patronage of the rulers of the pre-partition era as they were generally opposed to the freedom movement in undivided India. Most of them were from the areas now forming parts of Pakistan. When the division of the subcontinent became imminent they conveniently jumped on to the Muslim League band wagon. For instance, in Punjab, Pakistan's largest province, most of the feudal families supporting the pro-British Unionist Party, which opposed the freedom movement, found their members occupying leading positions in the Muslim League in the early days after Independence.

As against this, most members of the judiciary were drawn from the small but enlightened intelligentsia from the urban middle classes. People from this group found their voice in the affairs of the state through the civil service and independent professions like the Bar. Unlike their feudal counterparts, they had a greater benefit of liberal Western education and social values. Their interests were not tied to preserving an automatic feudal social order. They were more capable of appreciating the work of human rights, democratic values and the needs of the working people. In view of this background, when parliamentary leaders were hardly responsive to public opinion, the public had a great deal of expectation from the institution of the judiciary. The general perception seems to be that an average parliamentarian, by the very nature of his/her socio-economic background would be an autocrat, and this autocracy could only be checked by an enlightened judge who would stand up for democratic values and human rights. This attitude, on the part of both parliamentarians and judges, has given rise to judicial activism in Pakistan. I will cite a few of these cases in the later part of my paper.

Another historical reality is that the legislative power in our country was for a large number of years exercised by autocratic military regimes. Even when parliaments functioned, there have been few occasions when genuine debate and discussion or process of consultation has taken place before making laws on important issues. Most of the time, a draft Bill prepared by the bureaucracy has been handed down to colleagues by the parliamentary leader with a direction to support the same on the floor of parliament. Matters like constitutional amendments have been passed by parliament within minutes. Nevertheless, Pakistan is governed by a written constitution with guaranteed fundamental rights which enable the courts to strike down a law repugnant to such rights. These courts of law have come to the rescue of the nation by upholding the supremacy of the guaranteed fundamental rights over ordinary legislation. Some of the laws or parts of enactments which were declared void on account of inconsistency with fundamental rights provisions or on the grounds of discrimination are:

- sections 6(1)(c) and (g) and 29 of the Punjab Control of Goods Act 1951 (*Fazal Ahmed Ayubi v West Pakistan Province*);[1]

- section 23A and 23B of the Foreign Exchange Regulations Act 1947 (*Waris Meah v The State*);[2]

- the East Bengal State Acquisition Act 1950 (*Jubendra Kishore v The Province of East Pakistan*);[3]

---

1   PLD 1957 Lahore 388.
2   PLD 1957 SC 157.
3   PLD 1957 SC 9.

- section 7 of the Press (Emergency Powers) Act 1931 (*Mahmud Zaman v District Magistrate, Lahore*);[4]

- sections 3(1), 3A, B, C and 6(1) of the Political Parties Act 1962 (*Benazir Bhutto v Federation of Pakistan*);[5]

- section 6 of the Foreign Exchange (Prevention of Payments) Act 1972 (*Inamur Rehman v Federation of Pakistan and Others*);[6]

- Frontier Crimes Regulations 1901 (*Khan Abdul Akbar Khan v Deputy Commissioner, Peshawar*[7] and *Toti Khan v District Magistrate, Sibi*);[8]

- sections 6 and 7 of the West Pakistan Shops Establishment Ordinance 1969 (*Pakistan Barbers Association, Lahore v Province of Punjab*).[9]

One may refer to a few citations where the courts in Pakistan have upheld human rights over oppressive legislation. During 1965, when Pakistan was at war with India, legislation was made through an ordinance known as the 'The Defence of Pakistan Ordinance, 1965' whereby an executive functionary was given the power to order the detention of any citizen, after being satisfied that such detention was necessary for the purpose of the security of the state. The ordinance was immediately put to use. Some political leaders were detained whereafter they approached the High Courts seeking relief on the ground, *inter alia,* that there was no justification for ordering such detention. The argument raised on behalf of the state was that the Executive Officer/Deputy Commissioner had the sole prerogative to determine whether any detention was necessary and that such satisfaction of such officer could not be reviewed by the High Courts while exercising powers of judicial review. In a landmark judgment reported as *Malik Ghulam Jilani v Government of the West Pakistan*[10] the Supreme Court of Pakistan, by a majority decision, declined to follow the rule laid down by the House of Lords in the case of *Liversidge v Anderson*[11] and preferred the minority view of Lord Atkin holding that the subjective satisfaction test of the detaining authority was wrong and when the law empowered detention upon the satisfaction of the detaining authority, it meant that the authority should be satisfied on the objective ground which would persuade people to believe that such detention was necessary. After this judgment, the Defence of Pakistan Ordinance 1965 was amended and a new provision was introduced through which the provisions requiring satisfaction were changed to read as 'in the opinion of the detaining

---

4   PLD 1958 Lahore 651.
5   PLD 1988 SC 416.
6   1992 SCMR 563.
7   PLD 1957 Peshawar 100.
8   PLD 1957 Quetta 1.
9   PLD 1976 Lahore 769.
10   PLD 1967 SC 373.
11   [1942] AC 206.

authority'. In the case of *Government of West Pakistan v Begum Agha Abdul Karim Shorish Kashmiri*,[12] the detention under the amended law came up for consideration before the Supreme Court of Pakistan. It was held that, under Article 98 of the Constitution 1962 (now repealed) which conferred the power on the High Courts to issue a writ similar to *habeas corpus*, the court was required to satisfy itself that the detention was not without lawful authority or made in an unlawful manner. It was further observed that in view of the constitutional requirement, ordinary legislation purporting to allow detention on the basis of personal opinion of the detaining authority was only 'an exercise in futility' and that the mandate of the Constitution must prevail over the ordinary law and that it must be objectively established that the detention was necessary.

Now adverting to the aims and objects of the Harare Declaration which include the protection and promotion of the rule of law, the independence of the judiciary and just and honest government, it will be necessary, from the point of view of a Pakistani, that the public perception at large about judges and parliamentarians should be improved and all misgivings in the minds of the public about these two important organs of the State should be removed. This has become even more necessary because of the constitutional set-up of Pakistan where there are two sets of judiciary, one of the common law and second for the Shariah, that is, the Islamic Injunctions, based on the holy Qur'an and Sunnah. The superior judiciary as envisaged by the 1973 Constitution of Pakistan comprises three Courts; the Supreme Court; the High Courts of four Provinces; and the Federal Shariat Court.

Article 189 of the 1973 Constitution provides that all decisions of the Supreme Court are binding on all other courts in Pakistan whilst under Article 190, all executive and judicial authorities are required to act in aid of the Supreme Court. Likewise, Article 203-GG makes the decisions of the Federal Shariat Court binding on a High Court and all courts subordinate to a High Court. In this short background, one can see what should be the public perception in respect of the role to be played by the judges and parliamentarians and where a line is to be drawn limiting powers and jurisdiction of these two important organs of the State. In addition, there should be a mutuality of respect between the members of these two institutions.

How far courts can interfere in parliamentary matters was considered by a Full Bench of the Pakistan Supreme Court in *Pakistan v Amed Saeed Karim and Four Others*[13] where Justice AR Cornelius (as his Lordship then was) observed that if a proceeding of parliament is part of its integral proceedings and relates to its proper business, then it must be recognised as such by the courts and

---

12 PLD 1969 SC 14.
13 PLD 1958 SC 397.

they must refrain from interfering with it even based on the principle of justice, equity and good conscience. This view was followed by a Full Bench of the High Court of Sindh in *Karachi Bar Association v Abdul Hafeez Prizada and Another*[14] arising out of contempt proceedings. The question referred to Full Bench was answered in the affirmative, the court holding that the speeches of the members of the National Assembly enjoy qualified privilege subject to the Constitution and are amenable to contempt of court proceedings under Article 204 of the 1973 Constitution.

To conclude, the public perception in Pakistan with reference to the judiciary is that the people expect judges to rise to the occasion in order to protect and uphold their fundamental rights and protect them from the repressive laws enacted by parliament. Now the responsibilities of a Pakistani judge have multiplied by the introduction of the islamisation process, for courts are not competent to enforce a law which is contrary to the injunctions of Islam.

In the short history of Pakistan, the judiciary has, to a great extent, come up to the expectations of the down-trodden people. I referred earlier to a few of the landmark cases where the judges have righted a wrong. There are several other cases which, owing to paucity of time, I am unable to quote. In addition to these judgments, there is no parallel precedent in the legal history of any country where more than 11 judges of the Superior Courts refused to take a fresh oath after promulgation of the Provisional Constitutional Order, 1981 in place of the Constitutional 1973, by the military regime, which resulted in their automatic removal from the offices of the judgeship of the Supreme Court and High Courts. At the same time, the judges have endeavoured their best to preserve and uphold the supremacy of the parliament in Pakistan. The latest example is the case of *Mehr Zulfigar Ali Babu and Others v Government of Punjab and others*[15] where it was observed by a Full Bench of the Supreme Court 'that the court is not at liberty to inquire into the motives or *mala fide* on the part of legislature. Once a statute is competently made, the court is not entitled to question the wisdom or fairness of the legislature'. Nor can the court refuse to enforce a law competently made on the ground that the result would be to nullify its own judgment.

---

14   PLD 1988 Kar 309.
15   PLD 1997 SC 11.

APPENDICES

1   WORKING GROUP REPORTS

2   [A DRAFT] STATEMENT ON FREEDOM OF EXPRESSION
     FOR THE COMMONWEALTH

3   LIST OF PARTICIPANTS

4   BIOGRAPHIES OF SESSION LEADERS
     AND CONTRIBUTORS

5   THE FOUR SPONSORING ASSOCIATIONS

WORKING GROUP REPORTS

An integral part of the Colloquium was the holding of a series of working groups in which small numbers of participants were tasked with developing principles and ideas with a view to their eventual incorporation in the Guidelines. Several of these working groups produced quite detailed reports and these are reproduced below both as a useful record of the background to the development of the Guidelines themselves and also to elucidate the aims and objectives of some of the principles.

WORKING GROUP REPORT ON THE RELATIONSHIP BETWEEN PARLIAMENT AND THE JUDICIARY

Chair: David Amarti

Rapporteur: Anton Cooray

1   The legislative function is within the province of parliament. Judges can be creative in the interpretation of legislation, but must not usurp parliament's legislative function.

2   Judges must adopt a generous and purposive approach towards the interpretation of a Bill of Rights. This is particularly important in countries which are in the process of building democratic traditions. Judges have an important part to play in developing and maintaining a vibrant human rights environment throughout the Commonwealth.

3   Participants stressed the importance of human rights jurisprudence and international law in the interpretation of a Bill of Rights. They recognised that international human rights jurisprudence can greatly assist domestic courts in interpreting a Bill of Rights and it can also help expand the scope of a Bill of Rights by supplying its omissions.

Participants called upon Commonwealth countries to take speedy and effective steps towards implementing their international human rights obligations by enacting appropriate human rights legislation.

The importance was recognised of specialised legislation (such as equal opportunity laws) to extend the reach of a Bill of Rights to the private sphere.

4   Participants considered whether there was a need for any formal means of dialogue between the courts and the other two branches of government. A fear was expressed that any attempt to develop such a means of communication might encourage the exercise of undue influence over the judiciary. It was felt that different countries have different legitimate means for facilitating a sharing of various concerns. It was felt that whilst an exchange of views between the judiciary and the executive on policy matters was desirable, this should not provide any excuse to interfere with judicial independence.

5   Participants reaffirmed the fundamental premise that people should have unhindered and easy access to courts, particularly when seeking to enforce their fundamental human rights. To facilitate this, there was a need to remove, or at least ease, procedural obstacles on access to justice. It was also desirable to promote less formal forums for human rights dispute resolution, particularly human rights commissions, offices of the ombudsman and ADR mechanisms.

6   Participants were of the view that constitutional adjudication must belong to the ordinary courts of law. They recognised the importance of conferring special human rights jurisdiction on a superior court of law either exclusively or shared with other ordinary courts of law.

It was considered that the courts should enjoy the right to declare legislation to be unconstitutional and of no legal effect: although there may be circumstances where the appropriate remedy was for the court to declare the unconstitutionality of a statute and direct the legislature to take the necessary remedial legislative measures.

7   The importance of human rights education was recognised. Judges, lawyers, parliamentarians and academics alike needed to be kept fully informed of human rights developments.

WORKING GROUP REPORT ON ACCOUNTABILITY MECHANISMS

Chair: Paul East

Rapporteur: Kathleen Keating

1   Judicial accountability

(a) *Codes of conduct*

(1) A code of conduct should be considered by each judiciary as a means of ensuring accountability of judges.

(2) The Commonwealth Magistrates' and Judges' Association should be encouraged to carry to completion its Model Code of Judicial Conduct. The Association should also serve as a repository of codes of judicial conduct developed by Commonwealth jurisdictions which will serve as a resource-centre for other jurisdictions.

(b) *Enforcement provisions*

(1) The trend towards formal and more open mechanisms for dealing with complaints against judges was commented upon unfavourably. There was some agreement that formal mechanisms encourage non-meritorious complaints and erode confidence in the judiciary.

(2) It was proposed that where the penalty to be levied was anything short of removal, the disciplinary process should be informal and administered by the chief judge of the court. Public admonition of judges should be discouraged.

(3) Participants agreed that in cases where a judge was at risk of removal, the judge must have the right to be fully informed of the charges, to be represented at a hearing, to have the right to make a full defence and to be judged by an independent and impartial tribunal.

(c) *Grounds for dismissal*

(1) It was proposed that these should be limited to (i) inability to perform judicial duties; and (ii) misconduct.

Participants noted that in some cases, disciplinary processes were being used to deal with cases of disability due to causes such as senility or illness. It was felt that governments should be reminded of the necessity for the provision of appropriate pension and insurance schemes as a means of addressing these cases.

Participants noted with concern that whilst public criticism of judges was a legitimate means of ensuring accountability, in some jurisdictions the offence of scandalising the court was used to muzzle legitimate criticism.

(2) Participants agreed that governments should be reminded that the criminal law is not an appropriate mechanism for restricting legitimate criticism of the courts.

2 Parliamentary accountability

(a) *Accountability of the executive to parliament*

Members of the Working Group agreed the following:

(1) The Chair of the Public Accounts Committee must be appointed from the ranks of the opposition.

(2) The Auditor General must report directly to parliament.

(3) Offices of the Ombudsman should be encouraged as a means of promoting accountability

(4) Governments should be required to announce publicly, within a defined time period, their responses to reports of parliamentary committees.

(5) Standing orders should provide appropriate periods for questions by opposition members and opportunity for debate.

(b) *Accountability of individual members of parliament*

Members of the Working Group agreed the following:

(1) Conflict of interest guidelines should require full disclosure by members of parliament of their financial and business interests.

(2) Expulsion of members from parliament as a penalty for leaving their party (floor-crossing) should be viewed with caution as a possible infringement of members' independence.

(3) Referendums (citizens' initiatives), while promoted by some as a means of ensuring accountability, should be viewed with caution, as they can side-track the parliamentary agenda and dilute parliamentary accountability to the wider electorate.

(4) Laws allowing for the recall of members of parliament during their elected term of office should be viewed with caution as a potential threat to members' independence.

WORKING GROUP REPORT ON PRESERVING JUDICIAL INDEPENDENCE

Chair: David Amarti

Rapporteur: Colin Nicholls

Members of the Working Group agreed the following:

(a) *Judicial autonomy*

(1) Judicial Service Commissions (the commission) should be established with the duty of recommending candidates for judicial appointment to an appropriate officer of state (for example, President, Prime Minister or Minister of Justice).

(2) The commission should be appointed by a committee (the committee).

(3) The committee should be appointed on a principle of openness so far as the public are concerned. Its membership should be aimed to achieve independence. The committee might consist of the Chief Justice, heads of the jurisdiction, two senior legal practitioners from the private sector nominated by the Law Society or Bar Council and two lay persons nominated by the leaders of government, etc. Where appropriate, the Ministry of Justice should provide assistance to the committee. In larger jurisdictions it might consist of nine members. In smaller jurisdictions, it should not have less than three members.

(4) Candidates for appointment to the judiciary should be nominated by the commission itself and the government. It is important that there should be a wide pool to draw on from a diverse range of people. It is accepted that this may be difficult in small jurisdictions. The business of the commission should be conducted in private. Vacancies should be advertised to ensure there is a wide pool of people to draw on.

(5) The committee and commission should be creatures either of the constitution or statute.

(6) It is essential that the above proposals meet the needs of the individual jurisdiction.

(b) *Funding*

(1) A government ministry should provide funds to enable the judiciary to perform its functions to the highest judicial standards.

(2) It may be appropriate in some jurisdictions for an autonomous department to be established to administer the courts. This is important to ensure their independence

(3) Where an autonomous department is set up, the judiciary should control its budget through the department. The department's chief executive should draw up a budget and be accountable to parliament.

(c) *Training*

(1) Priority should be given to judicial training and education. A culture of judicial education should be developed.

(2) Training should be organised systematically and be ongoing. It should be under the control of a dedicated judicial body and sufficient funds should be provided to facilitate judicial training. In the case of those jurisdictions which do not have any funds or any adequate training facilities, access to facilities in other jurisdictions should be provided.

(3) Judicial officials should be in control of the curriculum. They should have the assistance of lay specialists in the provision of the programmes.

(4) Judicial training should include teaching of the law, judicial skills and the social context, for example, ethnic and gender issues.

WORKING GROUP REPORT ON GENDER BALANCING ISSUES

Chair: Sue Barnes

Rapporteur: Kamla Persad-Bissessar

(a) Women in parliament

(1) *Is gender balance necessary?*

Members of the Working Group agreed that increased gender balance is necessary to accomplish full and equal rights in society and there can be no true human rights without women's rights. Members noted that gender balance is mandated by many constitutions as well as regional and international human rights instruments.

The advantages of gender bodies were noted, especially the example of Scandinavian countries where the largest percentage of women parliamentarians is found and their impact is evident in the advanced nature of social legislation in those countries.

(2) *What constitutes adequate representation*

It was noted that the political process is a voluntary process and that to impose a quota system is to deny the voluntary nature of the political process. Thus, any Guidelines produced by the colloquium should not encourage a quota system but should look to the development of assistance and encouragement of women and the removal of constraints preventing women from joining parliament. It was noted that a 30% representation of women is generally accepted as a functional critical mass.

(3) *What are the constraints facing women seeking to join parliament?*

Members of the Group recognised that the two main barriers to women joining parliament are (i) attitudes and barriers of political parties; and (ii) the reluctance of women to offer themselves for political office: this was often a reflection of their culture or society.

The need to enhance the role of women within political parties was recognised and the Group noted that women fail to attain executive roles within their respective political parties and that this contributes to the inadequate representation of women in parliaments across the Commonwealth.

The lack of financial resources of women was recognised as a reason behind women's failure to offer themselves for political office together with both the perceptions and the reality of the impact of political office on family life.

(4) *How should these constraints be addressed?*

Members of the Group agreed the following:

- political parties in nations with proportional representation should be required to ensure an adequate gender balance on their respective lists of candidates for election. Women should be included in the top part of the candidate lists of political parties;

- parties should be called upon to publicly declare the degree of representation of women on their lists and to defend any failure to maintain adequate representation;

- proactive searches for potential candidates should be undertaken by political parties;

- where there is no proportional representation, candidate selection committees of political parties should be gender balanced as should representation of political conventions of parties when considering amendments to party constitutions;

- in nations where there is no proportional representation, women should be put forward for safe seats and not as 'sacrificial lambs' in constituencies where there is little likelihood of election;

- the provision of reservations for women in national constitutions whilst useful, tends to be insufficient for securing adequate and long-term representation by women. Women need to be elected to parliament through direct election;

- women need to be involved in the work of national law commissions as a routine step in the law-making process;

- as a routine step in the law-making process, legislation needs to be viewed through a gender lens to assess the impact of legislation on both genders. Gender neutral language in drafting and usage is appropriate.

- the need for universal access to education was recognised as was the current unequal access for many women and girl children. The educational process from nursery school to tertiary education should be reviewed to ensure that textbooks and teaching methods are gender balanced. Gender balance should be sought at every level from school debating societies to other forms of speaking sessions;

- organisers of conferences and colloquia should seek to attain a gender balance in their delegate lists. Men should also be involved in conferences on women's issues;

- men as partners need to be actively involved in and jointly responsible for redressing the gender imbalance in Commonwealth parliaments and societies. Men and women should act in partnership with one another to produce inclusive results. Women who have achieved power should seek to further the aim of gender balance in partnership with men.

(b) Women in the judiciary

(1) *Is gender balance necessary?*

The Group affirmed the points raised in Dame Silvia Cartwright's paper. It was recognised that gender balance is necessary to ensure the better administration of justice.

(2) *Constraints facing women seeking to join the judiciary*

Barriers to women becoming judges were recognised, including:

- social attitudes and constraints preventing women seeking judicial appointment;
- the appointment process not being gender balanced;
- insufficient women in senior judicial positions;
- insufficient education on gender issues for members of the Bar and judiciary;
- insufficient proactive search and solicitation of applicants to the judiciary.

(3) *How to address these constraints*

Members of the Group agreed the following:

- selection committees of judges and magistrates should be gender balanced;
- appointments to the judiciary should be on merit and gender balanced;
- search and solicitation of candidates for the judiciary should be proactive;
- it may be necessary to appoint women at a younger age;

- it may be necessary to allow the possibility of less circuit work for judges who request such accommodation;
- a ladder needs to be created to enable female judges to rise through the ranks to senior judicial and administrative posts;
- judicial training should be offered as part of the continuing professional development process of young practising lawyers and should not be restricted to post appointment.

(4) *Conclusions*

It was concluded that men should work in partnership with women to redress constraints on women entering parliament and the judiciary. Women should not be the sole custodians of women's and family issues. True gender balance requires the oppositional element of the inclusion of men in the process of dialogue and remedial action to address the necessary inclusion of both genders in all aspects of public life.

WORKING GROUP REPORT ON THE PARLIAMENTARY LAW-MAKING PROCESS

Chair: Sir Phillip M Bailhache

Rapporteur: John Dowd

(1) Procedures for the preliminary examination of issues in proposed legislation should be adopted and published so that:
- there is public exposure of issues papers and consultation on major reforms, including, where possible, a draft Bill;
- standing orders provide for some days delay between introduction and debate to enable public comment, unless suspended by consent or a significant high percentage vote of the chamber;
- major legislation should be referred to a select committee, preferably allowing the taking of evidence.

(2) Model standing orders should be settled and published internationally taking into account the size of the parliament and the number of chambers.

(3) Adequate resources to non-government and government back-benchers should be provided to improve parliamentary input. This should include:

- training for new members;
- adequate secretarial, accommodation and research facilities;
- drafting assistance.

(4) That appropriate legislation incorporates international human rights instruments to assist in interpretation and that Ministers certify compliance with such instruments, on introduction of the Bill.

(5) That 'sunset' legislation for the expiry of all subordinate legislation not renewed, be enacted.

(6) That, generally, there should be no contact in the law-making process or otherwise between the executive or parliamentarians with the judiciary unless with the approval of the head of the jurisdiction.

(7) Interpretation Acts should provide that, in interpreting statutes, reports, explanatory memoranda and parliamentary debates may be used.

[A DRAFT] STATEMENT ON FREEDOM OF EXPRESSION FOR THE COMMONWEALTH[1]

Freedom of expression is a universal human right. Freedom of expression is enshrined in many international and regional instruments, most notably the Universal Declaration of Human Rights and the International Covenant on Civil and Political Rights. Respect for freedom of expression inheres in the Commonwealth as an organisation and is implicit in the Harare Declaration of 1991 which recognises democracy, just and honest government and human rights as fundamental political values of the Commonwealth. The constitutions of many democratic states contain formally entrenched protection for freedom of expression.

While freedom of expression is a universal human right, the diversity of peoples and cultures that make up the Commonwealth must be acknowledged. Uniformity in the implementation and protection of freedom of expression is unnecessary. There is, nonetheless, a core of common principles at the heart of freedom of expression.

Freedom of expression means the freedom to receive and impart ideas, opinions and information without interference, hindrance or intimidation. It belongs to all persons and may be exercised through speaking, writing, publishing and broadcasting or through physical acts.

Freedom of expression is the primary freedom, an essential precondition to the exercise of other freedoms. It is the freedom upon which other rights and freedoms arise.

New technologies as well as developments in older technologies are transforming the practice of freedom of expression.

Freedom of expression is not licence. Freedom of expression may be limited in order to respect other social interests which are of pressing and substantial significance. Persons who exercise freedom of expression are under an obligation to do so responsibly and in a manner consistent with established ethical notions.

The principles that follow constitute a basis for the recognition of freedom of expression in a democratic legal system.

---

1   This is the more recent designation of the 'Commonwealth Statement on Freedom of Expression' referred to in Guidelines VIII, 1, p 27. The Statement itself is currently subject to further refinement, so the text should not be regarded as final. The Statement itself is the product of the Media Law Project set up by the Commonwealth Association for Education in Journalism and Communication (CAEJC).

(1) Ownership and Regulation of the Mass Media

There should be pluralism in the ownership and diversity in the content of the mass media. Pluralism will make it possible for a variety of voices to be heard.

While technology, especially in broadcasting, is changing rapidly, there should be separate legal regimes for the print and broadcasting media that reflect their different characteristics.

(a) Electronic media

The goal of pluralism is denied by monopoly ownership, whether on the part of the state or commercial interests. The balance to be achieved in a particular state will depend on the level of economic development in that state. State ownership of the broadcasting media does not necessitate government control of what is broadcast. State licensing of broadcasters is the norm in the world today. The licensing body should be autonomous and independent of direct government control. Licences must be awarded, denied, cancelled or suspended according to established and published criteria. The process of the licensing body must be open and non-discriminatory. It is legitimate for a state to establish criteria that deny broadcasting licences to non-citizens.

(b) Print media

The overriding goal of pluralism will be frustrated by monopoly ownership.

The licensing of newspapers, journals and magazines by the state is unacceptable.

The state may establish rules that limit the extent to which the same individuals or corporations may own both print and broadcasting media.

While it is legitimate for the state to own and produce a range of journals and publications, other printed publications, whether owned by individuals, corporations or institutions, should not be directly regulated by the state. Such publications may be subject to laws of general application that provide for the governance and control of businesses and private corporations.

(c) Foreign-owned mass media

It is legitimate for states to resist the homogenisation of the mass media. States may adopt measures designed to regulate the penetration of foreign broadcasting; there is no justification for imposing restrictions on the distribution of foreign newspapers or journals. The most efficacious means of protecting indigenous culture is through encouraging and supporting local broadcasting, rather than prohibiting or unduly restricting foreign broadcasting.

(d) Access

Legal rules that mandate general public access to the mass media are not necessary. Nonetheless, governments and media corporations should seek to encourage the presentation of diverse points of view. Governments should encourage and facilitate the development of community-based radio, television and newspapers.

A right of reply for opposing sides on controversial issues should be recognised and enforceable by law where persons establish their reputations have been damaged or that untrue information about them has been published. There should be a corresponding obligation on the mass media to correct errors and misstatements.

There should be formal rules that guarantee equitable access to the mass media for candidates and political parties during electoral campaigns.

(e) Administrative issues

The allocation of foreign exchange, the administration of import licensing, the imposition of taxation and the placing of government advertising can all be used in ways that limit freedom of expression and adversely affect the mass media. Such negative practices are unacceptable. On the other hand, positive practices such as tax advantages or the allocation of newsprint can be used in an affirmative fashion to benefit smaller, community-based broadcasters or publishers.

(2) Constitutional protection of freedom of expression

Freedom of expression should receive express, formal protection in written constitutions. This protection should reflect existing international human rights standards. Where this has not already happened, international human rights standards should be formally incorporated into national constitutions. If a new constitution is being adopted, or an older constitution is being revised, the guarantee of freedom of expression should be straightforward, direct and in non-technical language. Courts and governments should give effect to guarantees of freedom of expression in national constitutions and as provided by international law.

(3) Judicial proceedings and contempt of court

(a) Openness

Constitutional guarantees of rights should expressly recognise that, as a matter of principle, judicial proceedings are open to the public and to the mass media.

(b) Contempt of court

The law of contempt should be set out in statutory form in order to preclude arbitrariness and excessive use of judicial discretion.

In a democracy there is need for robust criticism of judicial decisions. The trend towards abandoning or narrowing the offence of scandalising the court is sound. Nevertheless, in extreme cases malicious and deliberate attacks on the judicial institution or on judges as members of the institution may be punished by the state.

It is also legitimate for the state to impose sanctions on media interference with the due administration of justice. Anyone accused of the offence of interference with the administration of justice must be accorded all the rights normally associated with criminal prosecutions. Furthermore, before anyone may be convicted of this offence, the prosecutor must prove that the accused created a real and substantial risk of prejudice to the outcome of a proceeding actually before the courts.

(c) Protection of journalists' sources

The question of the possible revelation by a journalist called as a witness in a judicial proceeding of information received in confidence from a source raises a conflict between two public interests. These interests are freedom of expression and the free circulation of information, on the one hand, and the integrity of the judicial process, which depends on all relevant and necessary information being available to a court, on the other. A broad discretion should be given to judges to balance these interests. In exercising this discretion, judges should avoid requiring any unnecessary revelation of confidential information. Among the factors a judge should consider are the seriousness of the matter before the court, the possibility of harm to the source or the journalist, and the general effect on sources of information. The more open is the flow of information in a society, the less the need for journalists to rely on confidential sources.

(d) Searches of newsrooms

Searches of media newsrooms can have a chilling effect on freedom of expression. Such searches should be permitted only pursuant to a warrant issued by a judicial officer in accordance with established law. A warrant for the search of a newsroom should be issued only as a last resort and may permit the persons executing it to search only for specified items.

(4) State security and public order

(a) Security issues

The constitutional authority to declare a state of emergency should not be exercised unless, in the words of the International Covenant on Civil and Political Rights, the 'life of the nation' is threatened. The use of colonial emergency provisions is to be deplored. Existing colonial emergency laws should be replaced. New legislation should conform to international law. Emergency powers must never be used as a substitute for the normal system of government. States of emergency should be rare and they should be brief. Preventive detention should be permitted only pursuant to a formal declaration of an emergency.

The journalist, operating in good faith, should not become the object of emergency laws or other public security provisions. But the journalist who ceases to operate as a journalist and becomes an activist or partisan must be prepared to accept full responsibility for such behaviour.

The law of criminal libel, if not already repealed, should only be used to protect public order, it should not be used to control expression.

The objective of promoting relations with friendly states is not a legitimate basis for limiting free expression.

(b) State information issues

The practice of government secrecy is a relic of earlier times. The goal should be to achieve maximum openness in government. Where it does not exist, access to information legislation should be enacted. Such legislation will recognise access to information as a basic principle. Limits on access should be few and carefully defined. The monetary costs of access to information should be reasonable. There should be independent review of refusals to permit access.

(5) The journalist as employee

Free expression does not belong exclusively to employers and managers. Rather, free expression requires that journalists enjoy substantial professional independence. The terms of employment of journalists should respect and reflect this requirement.

Freedom of expression demands the recognition of journalists' professional associations and unions. Journalists' unions play an essential role in protecting journalists and advancing professional standards.

(6) Protecting social values and social groups

Most Commonwealth countries are multicultural, which is to say they contain a multiplicity of cultural, ethnic, linguistic or religious groups. The mass media can be a positive force in promoting harmony in such societies, but they can also be a negative force and promote hostility and hatred. Journalists in multicultural societies bear special responsibilities for the way they exercise their freedom of expression.

It is legitimate for the state to suppress and to use criminal sanctions against public statements which can be proved to be promotion or advocacy of hatred or incitement to violence on the basis of race, religion, ethnic or linguistic group membership, sex or sexual orientation.

It is not legitimate for the state to prohibit or limit the public or private use of any language.

The law with respect to obscenity and pornography must arise from and respect the values of the society in which it operates. States have a special responsibility for eliminating child pornography.

The offence of blasphemy or blasphemous libel should be repealed or restricted in its scope. The state may limit the public denigration of religious beliefs, but it should not interfere with the discussion of religious beliefs.

Journalists should establish professional codes and standards governing these matters.

The media and advertisers should develop codes that establish standards for advertising.

(7) Private rights

(a) Civil defamation

We do not favour fundamental reform in the law of defamation. The law should continue to strike an appropriate balance between the protection of reputation and freedom of expression. Commonwealth states should not follow the direction taken in the United States of offering special protection to those who defame so-called 'public figures' unless there is proof of malice. While open criticism of public figures is healthy and desirable, we believe that the US approach leads to bad journalism, civic unfairness and unfair and unreasonable attacks on people in public life.

Some reforms are desirable. There should be consideration of new remedies in defamation actions, including correction and a right to reply. Where damages are to be awarded, the awards should be moderate and consistent. Speed and expedition in the resolution of defamation actions should be encouraged and serious efforts should be made to reduce their costs and technicality. Finally, government departments and ministries, state corporations and parastatals should not have the legal capacity to sue as plaintiffs in defamation actions.

(b) Privacy

A feature of contemporary media practice is intrusion into what should be the private lives of individuals, especially persons who are neither officials nor public figures. The law has so far failed to address this situation adequately. This must be rectified. In particular, intrusions by reporters and photographers and the hounding of persons targeted by the mass media should be regulated. At the same time, respect for the privacy of individuals should be reflected in journalists' codes of ethics.

(8) Public accountability and the mass media

(a) Press Councils

The establishment of Press Councils is to be encouraged. Press Councils need to be strengthened and should encourage the trend towards media self-regulation.

The tripartite model, structured around separate and distinct interests of the public, journalists and media owners or managers is to be preferred. Press Councils should not be the forum, however, for the resolution of purely employer-employee disputes.

(b) Code of Ethics

Journalism should remain an unregulated profession. The adoption of Codes of Ethics should be encouraged. Such codes should be created and administered by journalists, not by the state.

Amongst other matters, Codes of Ethics must require that journalists maintain high standards of integrity, honesty and accuracy; avoid disinformation; steadfastly refuse to be manipulated by or become propagandists for governments, corporations or political or other interests; and scrupulously maintain the distinction between presenting facts and presenting opinions.

A unique set of challenges to journalistic ethics and practices arises when journalists confront terrorism or armed insurgency. Journalists may become targets both in order to achieve publicity and to prevent the objective reporting of events. New legal and professional responses to these realities must be fashioned.

(c) Offices of the Ombudsman

The spread of the institution of internal media offices of the ombudsman should be encouraged. The practical value of an ombudsman lies in promoting the resolution of disputes between the media and their readers, listeners and viewers.

LIST OF PARTICIPANTS

COMMONWEALTH LAWYERS' ASSOCIATION PARTICIPANTS

Mr David Anderson
    CLA Council Member/Solicitor
    Scotland

Dr Rodger Chongwe, SC
    CLA Past President and former Minister of Legal Affairs
    Zambia

Dr Cyrus Das
    President of the Bar Council
    Malaysia

Mr Rodney Hansen, QC
    CLA President
    New Zealand

Ms Kathleen Keating
    CLA Council Member
    Canada

Mr Colin Nicholls, QC
    CLA Honorary Treasurer
    England and Wales

Lt Col Hurlstone St Clair Whitehorne
    CLA Past President
    Jamaica

Shri Soli J Sorabjee
    Attorney General
    India

Staff

Ms Helen Potts (nee Ramsey)
    CLA Assistant Executive Secretary

COMMONWEALTH LEGAL EDUCATION
ASSOCIATION PARTICIPANTS

Professor Shaheen Sadar Ali
    University of Peshawar
    Pakistan

Professor Anton Cooray
    City University of Hong Kong
    Sri Lanka

Ms Sarah Hossain
    Interights
    United Kingdom

Professor Robert Martin
    University of Western Ontario
    Canada

Mr Lawrence Mute
    Centre for Law and Research International
    Kenya

Professor Dawn Oliver
    University College London
    United Kingdom

Professor James S Read
    Past CLEA Chairman
    United Kingdom

Mr Keith Sobion
    CLEA Executive Committee Member
    Jamaica

Dr Nik Nozrul Thani Nik Hassan Thani
  Vice President, CLEA
  Malaysia

Staff

Dr Peter Slinn
  Vice President, CLEA/School of Oriental and African Studies, University of London

John Hatchard
  General Secretary, CLEA/School of Oriental and African Studies, University of London

COMMONWEALTH MAGISTRATES' AND JUDGES' ASSOCIATION PARTICIPANTS

Mr David Armati
  President, CMJA
  Australia

Hon Justice Mary Arden, DBE
  Chair of the Law Commission
  United Kingdom

Hon Chief Justice Richard Banda
  Chief Justice and Member of the CMJA Council
  Malawi

Hon Justice Dame Silvia Cartright
  Judge of the High Court
  New Zealand

Hon Justice John Dowd, AO
  Judge of the Supreme Court
  Australia

Hon Chief Justice Anthony Gubbay
  Chief Justice
  Zimbabwe

Hon Justice KM Nagabhushan Rao
    District Judge and Council Member, CMJA
    India

Hon Justice Pierré Olivier
    Justice of the Supreme Court of Appeal
    South Africa

Hon Justice Rasheed Razvi
    Justice, High Court of Sindh
    Pakistan

Hon Chief Justice Derek Schofield
    Chief Justice
    Gibralter

Staff

Mr Michael A Lambert
    Executive Vice President and Honorary Treasurer CMJA

Dr Karen Brewer
    Secretary General

COMMONWEALTH PARLIAMENTARY ASSOCIATION PARTICIPANTS

Shri E Ahmed, MP
    India

Mr Nana Addo Dankwa Akufo-Addo, MP
    Shadow Minister of Justice
    Ghana

Senator Raynell Andreychuck
    Canada

Ms Susan Barnes, MP
    Canada

Sir Phillip M Bailhache
  Bailiff of Jersey and President of the States
  Jersey

Mrs Rabia Bhuiyan, MP
  Bangladesh

Mr NM Chibesakunda
  Clerk of the National Assembly
  Zambia

Rt Hon Paul East, QC, MP
  New Zealand

Dr the Hon HA Fergus, CBE, MLC
  Speaker of the Legislative Council
  Montserrat

Hon Peter McGauran, MP
  Australia

Hon Kamla Persad-Bissessar, MP
  Minister of Legal Affairs
  Trinidad and Tobago

Mr Wasim Sajjad
  Chairman of the Senate
  Pakistan

Hon Misa Telefoni, MP
  Minister of Health
  Samoa

Staff

Mr Arthur Donahoe, QC
  Secretary General

Ms Meenakshi Dhar
  Assistant Director

Mr Shem Baldeosingh
  Information Officer

Other invitees

Mr Richard Bourne
    Commonwealth Human Rights Initiative (CHRI)

Mr Derek Ingram
    Commonwealth Journalists Association/CHRI

Professor Peter Lyon
    Institute of Commonwealth Studies

Ms Christine Mulindwa-Matovu
    Head, Human Rights Unit
    Commonwealth Secretariat

Mr Richard Nzerem
    Director, Legal and Constitutional Affairs Division
    Commonwealth Secretariat

BIOGRAPHIES OF SESSION LEADERS AND CONTRIBUTORS

Mr Nana Addo Dankwa Akufo-Addo, MP

Ghana

Mr Addo was called to the English Bar (Middle Temple) in 1971 and to the Ghanaian Bar in 1975. From 1971–75, he was Associate Counsel to a United States law firm, Coudert Brothers, at its Paris office. In 1979, he was co-founder of the law firm Akufo-Addo, Prempeh & Co.

He was General Secretary of the People's Movement for Freedom and Justice (1977–78). Between 1989 and 1991, he was Vice President of the Accra Regional Branch of the Ghana Bar Association and its President from 1991–96. He was also a Member of the General Legal Council and Member of the Legal Committee of the Ghana Bar Association (1991–96).

He was the first Chairman of the Ghana Committee on Human and Peoples' Rights between 1992 and 1998 and was a Member of the National Council and the National Executive Committee of the New Patriotic Party (NPP). He has also served as Secretary of the Legal and Constitutional Affairs Committee, Political Committee and Policy Advisory Committee of the NPP.

He was elected MP for the Abuakwa constituency in 1996. Since then he has served as Chairman of the parliamentary Standing Committee on Subsidiary Legislation and as the Ranking Minority Member on the parliamentary Select Committee on Constitutional, parliamentary and Legal Affairs. He is also the minority spokesperson for the Alliance for Change, a broad-based political pressure group.

Sir Phillip M Bailhache

Jersey

Sir Philip is a member of the Middle Temple and called to the English Bar in 1968. He was admitted to the Jersey Bar in 1969. In 1972, he was elected to the States of Jersey as Deputy of Grouville. He resigned as Deputy upon his appointment as Solicitor General for Jersey in 1975.

In 1986, he was appointed Attorney General for Jersey and in 1989 was made Queen's Council. In 1994, he was appointed Deputy Bailiff and in 1995 became Bailiff of Jersey. He was knighted in 1996.

Ms Susan Barnes, MP

Canada

Ms Barnes was admitted to the Law Society of Canada in 1979 and was a self-employed full time lawyer between 1979 and 1993. During part of this period, she served as a part time Legal Member of the Ontario Criminal Code Review Board. Between 1982 and 1986, she was a Instructor in Business Law and Banking Law at the University of Western Ontario.

Ms Barnes has served as the MP for London West since 1993. She has served as parliamentary Secretary to the Minister of National Revenue since February 1996 and was the government Vice Chairperson of the Standing Committee on Justice and Legal Affairs between 1994 and 1996.

She was a member of the executive Committee of the Canadian Inter-Parliamentary Union (IPU) between 1994 and 1996 and participated in IPU conferences in Copenhagen, Bucharest and Beijing during this time. She also chaired the Drafting Committee on Corruption at the 94th IPU Conference in Bucharest in October 1995.

Hon Justice Dame Silvia Cartright

New Zealand

During her judicial career, Dame Silvia served as Chief Judge of the District Courts before her appointment to the High Court.

She is a member of the United Nations Committee which monitors compliance with the Convention on the Elimination of All Forms of Discrimination against Women.

She recently also chaired a symposium for the entire New Zealand judiciary on gender issues and the judiciary.

Dr Rodger Chongwe, SC

Zambia

Rodger Chongwe is a former Minister of Legal Affairs and a former Minister of Local Government and Housing in the government of the Republic of Zambia. He is a founder member of the Movement for Multi-Party Democracy and was formerly a member of parliament in Zambia. A lawyer by profession, he runs the law firm RMA Chongwe and Company which he established in 1977.

He held the post of Secretary and then President of the Commonwealth Lawyers' Association from 1986 to 1993. He was President of the African Bar Association from 1985–91 and Chairperson of the Law Association of Zambia.

Professor Anton Cooray

Sri Lanka

Anton Cooray is a former Head and Dean of the University of Colombo's Law School. He is currently on the law department of the City University of Hong Kong where he was Head of the Department of Law between 1995 and 1997.

His special interests are constitutional and administrative law, legal systems and land-use and planning law.

Dr Cyrus V Das

Malaysia

Cyrus Das is Senior Partner at Messrs Shook Lin & Bok in Kuala Lumpur. He is currently President of the Bar Council of Malaysia and Honorary Secretary of the Commonwealth Lawyers' Association.

He is also co-chair of the Constitutional Law Standing Committee of LAWASIA and Vice President of the Asean Law Association.

Mr Arthur Donahoe, QC

Mr Donahoe was born and educated in Halifax, Nova Scotia. He is a Barrister and Solicitor and in 1982 was appointed a Nova Scotia Queen's Counsel. He was a member of the Nova Scotia Legislature from 1978–92 and served as Speaker of the House of Assembly from 1981–91.

Since 1993, he has been Secretary General of the Commonwealth Parliamentary Association, an organisation of over 14,000 Parliamentarians in 142 Parliaments and Legislatures in 50 Commonwealth countries. He is the Association's CEO, responsible for the interpretation and implementation of its programmes and policies and is in charge of the CPA Secretariat, located in London.

Rt Hon Paul East, QC, MP

New Zealand

Paul East was admitted as a Barrister and Solicitor of the Supreme Court of New Zealand in 1971. He was appointed Queen's Counsel in 1995. From 1978–96, he was the MP for Rotorua. From 1990, he was Chair of the Privileges Committee, House of Representatives.

He served at various times as Opposition Spokesman for Commerce and Customs, Justice, Constitutional Affairs and Health. He was appointed Attorney General and Leader of the House in 1990 and was responsible for the legal representation of the government and the appointment of judges to the High Court and Court of Appeal. He was later appointed Minister responsible for the Serious Fraud Office and the Audit Department and in October 1991 was appointed Minister for Crown Health Enterprises. In 1993, he was appointed Minister of State Service.

In January 1996, he was appointed Minister of Defence and Minister of Corrections. In December 1996, he was appointed to the Coalition government Cabinet as Attorney General, Minister of State Service, Minister of Defence, Minister of Corrections and Minister responsible for the Serious Fraud Office.

Since 1990, he has been a Member of the Permanent Court of Arbitration in The Hague.

The Hon Chief Justice Anthony Gubbay

Zimbabwe

Chief Justice Gubbay was admitted to practice in South Africa in 1957. He emigrated to Southern Rhodesia (as it then was) in March 1958 and commenced practice as an advocate. He was appointed Senior Counsel in 1974, Judge of the High Court in 1977, Judge of the Supreme Court in 1983 and Chief Justice in 1990.

He was elected as an Honorary Fellow of Jesus College, Cambridge in 1992, awarded an Honorary Doctorate by the University of Essex in 1994 and was made an Honorary Bencher of Lincoln's Inn in 1998.

Mr Rodney Hansen, QC

New Zealand

Rodney Hansen was admitted to the Bar in 1969 and was a partner with Simpson Grierson Butler & White, Barristers and Solicitors between 1979 and 1991. He has been a Barrister Sole since 1991 and was appointed Queen's Counsel in 1995.

He has been a council member of the Commonwealth Lawyers' Association since 1986, served as Hon Secretary between 1993–96 and, since 1996, has been the President of the CLA.

John Hatchard

John Hatchard is General Secretary of the Commonwealth Legal Education Association and Editor of Commonwealth Legal Education, the Newsletter of the Association.

He is a Barrister of the Middle Temple. He has taught law at universities in Zambia, Zimbabwe, the United States and the United Kingdom and is currently a Visiting Reader at the School of Oriental and African Studies, University of London. He was formerly Chief Mutual Legal Assistance Officer at the Commonwealth Secretariat.

He has written widely on comparative public law issues, especially with regard to Commonwealth Africa. He is also Joint Editor of the *Journal of African Law*.

Baron Irvine of Lairg

The Lord High Chancellor of Great Britain

The Right Honourable the Lord Irvine of Lairg was invited to become Lord High Chancellor of Great Britain on 2 May 1997.

He was a lecturer in law at the London School of Economics from 1965–69 and called to the Bar by the Inner Temple in 1967. He became a QC in 1978. He served as a Recorder from 1985–88 and was appointed a Deputy High Court Judge in 1987. He ceased to practice on becoming Lord Chancellor.

Since being appointed Lord Chancellor, he has also become Joint President of the Commonwealth Parliamentary Association, UK Branch, President of the Magistrates' Association and Joint President of the Inter-Parliamentary Union. He is also an Honorary Fellow of the Society for Advanced Legal Studies and Vice Patron of the World Federation of Mental Health.

Ms Kathleen Keating

Canada

Kathleen Keating is a recent appointee to the British Columbia Treaty Commission, a five-member body established by the Canadian and BC governments and the First Nation Summit to monitor, facilitate and administer the negotiation of modern-day treaties.

In her consulting practice, she advises government and professional bodies in matters of plain language drafting, administrative law and court procedure.

She has been a council member of the CLA since 1993.

Professor Robert Martin

Canada

Robert Martin has held the position of Professor of Law at the University of Western Ontario since 1978. He was admitted as a Barrister and Solicitor to the Ontario Bar in 1978 and was made a Bencher of the Law Society of Upper Canada in 1997.

He has been the Treasurer of the Commonwealth Association for Education in Journalism and Communication since 1985 and the Director of the Commonwealth Media Laws Project since 1995.

Hon Peter McGauran, MP

Australia

Peter McGauran worked as a Barrister and Solicitor prior to being elected to the Federal parliament in March 1983 at the age of 27 years. He has since been re-elected on four subsequent occasions.

He has served on various parliamentary committees including the committee overseeing the Australian Securities Intelligence Organisation and the committee overseeing the National Crime Authority.

He served as Shadow Minister for Science and Technology between 1988 and 1993 and as Shadow Minister for Resources and Energy between 1993 and 1996. Between March 1996 and September 1997, he served as Minister for Science and Technology.

Mr Colin Nicholls, QC

United Kingdom

Colin Nicholls was called to the Bar in 1957 and appointed a Queen's Counsel in 1981. He was elected a Bencher of Gray's Inn in 1990. He also serves as a Recorder in the Crown Courts.

His principal areas of practice relate to commercial crime, extradition and civil liberties.

He was Vice President of the Commonwealth Lawyers' Association between 1985 and 1996 and the Hon Treasurer between 1996 and 1998. He is a member of the Bar European Group, the British Institute of International and Comparative Law, the Criminal Bar Association, the European Criminal Bar Association and has been admitted ad hoc to the Bar of Hong Kong.

Professor Dawn Oliver

United Kingdom

Dawn Oliver is Professor of Constitutional Law in the University of London at University College London. She is Dean of the Faculty of Laws and Head of Department. She is a Bencher of the Middle Temple.

She has been Editor of *Public Law* since 1994. Her special interests include constitutional and public service reform and the public law-private law divide.

Among her publications are: *Government in the United Kingdom: The Search for Accountability, Effectiveness and Citizenship* (1991) and the Fourth Edition reissue of *Halsbury's Laws of England: Constitutional Law and Human Rights* with Lord Lester of Herne Hill, QC (1997).

Hon Justice Pierré Olivier

South Africa

Justice Olivier was formerly a law professor during which time he authored and co-authored standard textbooks on the law of delict, the law of persons and family law.

In 1973, he joined the Bar and practised as an advocate until 1985 when he was elected to the High Court Bench. Seconded to the South African Law Commission in 1986, he was the author of the Commission's report on human rights which played a significant role in moving South Africa away from apartheid and towards the acceptance of a justiciable Bill of Rights.

He was appointed to the Supreme Court of Appeal in 1995.

Hon Kamla Persad-Bissessar, MP

Trinidad and Tobago

Originally a legal practitioner in her own law chambers, Ms Persad-Bissessar became a member of parliament and then in 1995 became the first woman ever to be appointed Attorney General and Minister of Legal Affairs of the Republic of Trinidad and Tobago.

In 1997, she was instrumental in achieving the monumental task of updating Trinidad and Tobago's companies legislation with a new Companies Act. She has chaired several parliamentary committees, a Joint Select Committee on the Office of the Ombudsman and an ad hoc committee that examined and made extensive recommendations for the reform of the Domestic Violence Act 1991.

Hon Justice KM Nagabhushan Rao

India

Justice Nagabhushan Rao practised at the Bar for 10 years before being appointed as a District and Sessions Judge.

He is a member of the Commonwealth Magistrates' and Judges' Association and on its Executive Council for the Indian Ocean region.

He has worked as a consultant to the United Nations Commissioner for Refugees. He has also written several articles on legal topics.

Hon Justice Rasheed Razvi

Pakistan

Justice Razvi joined the legal profession in 1972. He was enrolled as an advocate of the subordinate courts in 1973 and as an advocate of the High Court in 1987. He was elected General Secretary of the Karachi Bar Association in 1981 and 1992.

He was appointed Special Judge for Officers in Banks for the Province of Sindh in 1993. He was elevated to be a judge of the High Court in 1995 and was confirmed as a puisne judge at the High Court of Sindh.

Professor James S Read

United Kingdom

Until his retirement in 1996, James Read was Professor of Comparative Public Law, with special reference to Africa, in the University of London at the School of Oriental and African Studies. He has been Emeritus Professor (with the same title) since that date.

He was the Chairman of the Commonwealth Legal Education Association between 1977 and 1983. He has co-authored two books and written various articles on the laws and constitutions of Commonwealth states, mainly in Africa. He remains Joint General Editor of the Law Reports of the Commonwealth.

At various times, he has been a consultant/advisor to several Commonwealth African states and has served as an external examiner in nine African countries.

Mr Wasim Sajjad

Pakistan

Mr Sajjad is a Barrister who has appeared in a large number of cases of constitutional importance before the High Court of Pakistan. Between 1967 and 1977, he also lectured on constitutional law at the University Law College, Lahore. He is an Honorary Fellow of Wadham College, Oxford.

He held the office of Minister for Justice and parliamentary Affairs from September 1986 to December 1988. In December 1988, he was elected as Chairman of the Senate of Pakistan.

From July to November 1993, he served as President of Pakistan.

Hon Chief Justice Derek Schofield

Gibraltar

Justice Schofield is a member of Gray's Inn having been called to the Bar in 1970. He was stationed in Kenya from 1974–87 holding various judicial offices including that of Senior Resident Magistrate and Judge Advocate to the Kenyan Navy.

In 1982, he was elevated to the High Court of Kenya before resigning in 1987. Between 1988 and 1996, he served as Judge of the Grand Court of the Cayman Islands before taking up the post of Chief Justice, Gibralter, in February 1996. In 1997, he was appointed an Assistant Recorder for the South Eastern Circuit in England.

Dr Peter Slinn

United Kingdom

Peter Slinn is joint Vice President of the Commonwealth Legal Education Association. He qualified as a solicitor (England and Wales) in 1967 when he joined the United Kingdom Diplomatic Service as an Assistant Legal Adviser. He subsequently left the Diplomatic Service to pursue an academic career, completing a London University doctoral thesis in 1974. Since 1977, he has been a member of the Law Department of the School of Oriental and African Studies, where he teaches international law and diplomacy, law and development and comparative constitutional law. He is currently Academic Director of the School's Postgraduate Programme in International Studies and Dipomacy. He is Joint General Editor of the *Law Reports of the Commonwealth*, Joint Editor of the *Journal of African Law* and a member of the editorial boards of the *African Journal of International and Comparative Law*, *The Commonwealth Judicial Journal* and *The Commonwealth Lawyer*.

Shri Soli Jehangir Sorabjee

India

Shri Sorabjee commenced legal practice in 1955 and was enroled as a Senior Advocate, Supreme Court of India in 1971. He served as Solicitor General of India between 1971 and 1980 and was Attorney General for India between 1989 and 1990, a position he resumed in 1998.

He has been President, United Lawyers' Association, Chairperson, Commonwealth Human Rights Initiative (India), Chairman, Advisory Board, Transparency International (India), Vice President, Human Rights Committee of the International Bar Association, Vice President, Commonwealth Lawyers' Association, Member of the Advisory Commission, Commonwealth Human Rights Initiative and Honorary Professor of Law, National Law School of

India, Bangalore. In October 1997, he was appointed by the United Nations Human Rights Commission as Special Rapporteur to report to the UN General Assembly on the human rights situation in Nigeria.

THE FOUR SPONSORING ASSOCIATIONS

 COMMONWEALTH LAWYERS'
ASSOCIATION

c/o The Law Society, 113 Chancery Lane,
London WC2A 1PL, UK

Fax: +44 (0) 171 831 0057

e-mail: helen.potts@lawsociety.org.uk

Office bearers

President: Rodney Hansen, QC

Honorary Secretary: Dr Cyrus Das

Executive Secretary: Helen Potts

Structure

The CLA operates under a Constitution which was formally adopted in September 1986. It has a Council of distinguished lawyers from around the Commonwealth.

All the more than 100 Law Societies and Bar Associations of the Commonwealth are institutional members of the CLA. The Association also has hundreds of individual members. Membership is open to any qualified lawyer in the Commonwealth.

An application form for individual membership can be obtained from the Secretariat of the CLA at the above address or by e-mail at:

e-mail: Nankunda.Katangaza@lawsociety.org.uk

Aims

The purpose of the Commonwealth Lawyers' Association is to maintain and promote the rule of law throughout the Commonwealth by ensuring that the people of the Commonwealth are served by an independent and efficient legal profession; by ensuring that a common bond of Commonwealth is preserved and fostered; by the strengthening of professional links between members of the legal profession; by the maintenance of the honour and integrity of the profession and the promotion of uniformity in the standards of professional ethics; and by the encouragement of improved standards of education and the promotion of exchanges of lawyers and students.

Activities

The CLA sponsors and plays a large part in the organisation of the Commonwealth Law Conferences, which are hosted, usually on a triennial basis, by the legal profession of a Commonwealth country. The Bar Council of Malaysia is host to the 12th Commonwealth Law Conference in Kuala Lumpur in September 1999. The Law Society of Zimbabwe is host to the 13th Commonwealth Law Conference in Harare in September 2001.

Other activities include: training sessions and workshops for lawyers and Law Society and Bar Council staff and representatives in developing Commonwealth countries; participation at and lobbying of Commonwealth Heads of Government and Commonwealth Law Ministers' Meetings; participation in fact-finding missions; support of a programme to recover surplus law books in England and Wales and to ship them to parts of the Commonwealth where they are most needed (Book Aid International); holding competitions for young lawyers from across the Commonwealth; and a major project on the transferability of legal qualifications in the Commonwealth.

The CLA is also a founder member of the Commonwealth Human Rights Initiative which promotes adherence to international and domestic human rights standards throughout the Commonwealth.

Publications

The CLA keeps in contact with its members through its quarterly newsletter *Clarion*.

COMMONWEALTH LEGAL EDUCATION ASSOCIATION

c/o Legal and Constitutional Affairs Division, Commonwealth Secretariat, Marlborough House, Pall Mall, London SW1Y 5HX, UK

Tel: +44 (0) 171 747 6415

Fax: +44 (0) 171 747 6406/636 5615

e-mail: jh10@soas.ac.uk

Office bearers

President: David McQuoid-Mason (University of Natal, Durban)

Vice Presidents: Peter Slinn (School of Oriental and African Studies); Keith Sobion (Norman Manley Law School, Jamaica); and Nik Nozrul Thani Nik Hassan Thani (Malaysia)

General Secretary: John Hatchard

Foundation

The CLEA was formed in December 1971. It is recognised as a charity by the UK Charity Commissioners and receives funding from the Commonwealth Foundation as well as from other sources.

Structure

The Association operates under a Constitution which was revised in 1993.

The Association is run by an Executive Committee representing all regions of the Commonwealth. In addition to the office bearers noted above, the current Committee comprises: Lillian Tibatemwa-Ekirikubinza (Makerere University, Uganda: responsible for East Africa); NL Mitra (National Law School of India University: responsible for South Asia); Seth Bimpong-Buta (Ghana Law School: responsible for West Africa); Robert Fowler (University of Adelaide: responsible for Australasia and the Pacific) and Richard Nzerem (Hon Treasurer).

Aims

Its objects are to foster high standards of legal education and research in Commonwealth countries; to build up contacts between interested individuals and organisations; and to disseminate information and literature concerning legal education and research.

Membership is open to individuals, schools of law and other institutions concerned with legal education and research. It enjoys the support of a distinguished list of patrons from around the Commonwealth. It has regional Chapters in South Asia and in Southern Africa.

Activities

- Holding regular workshops and conferences. In recent years, these have been held in South Africa (1995), Malaysia (1997) and Jamaica (1998)
- Organising the Commonwealth Law Students Mooting Competition at Commonwealth Law Conferences
- Participating in the Commonwealth Law Book programme
- Developing a Programme of Action entitled *Legal Education in the Commonwealth: The Way Ahead* designed to achieve sustainable improvements in legal education throughout the Commonwealth
- Holding regular essay competitions for Commonwealth law students
- Facilitating visits and exchanges for faculty members in Commonwealth law schools

The CLEA is a founder member of the Commonwealth Human Rights Initiative which promotes adherence to international and domestic human rights standards throughout the Commonwealth and is involved in the work of Book Aid International.

Publications

- *Commonwealth Legal Education*, the Newsletter of the Association (three issues per year)
- *Directory of Commonwealth Law Schools* (every two years)

COMMONWEALTH MAGISTRATES' AND JUDGES' ASSOCIATION

Uganda House, 58–59 Trafalgar Square, London WC2N 5DX, UK

Tel: +44 (0) 171 976 1007

Fax: +44 (0) 171 976 2395

e-mail: cmja@btinternet.com

Office bearers

President: Mr David Armati

Executive Vice President: Mr MA Lambert

Secretary General: Dr Karen Brewer

Foundation

The CMJA was formed in 1970 as the Commonwealth Magistrates' Association, and changed to its current name in 1988. It is a registered charity.

Structure

The main governing body of the Association is the General Assembly of its members which meets at least every four years. Between meetings its affairs are conducted by an elected council, which meets annually, with representatives of the six regions: Caribbean, East and Central Africa, West Africa, Indian Ocean, North Atlantic and Mediterranean, and Pacific Ocean.

Aims

The CMJA links magistrates and judges in Commonwealth countries to assist them to advance the administration of justice.

- To advance the administration of the law by promoting the independence of the judiciary.

- To advance education in the law, the administration of justice, the treatment of offenders and the prevention of crime.
- To disseminate information and literature on matters of interest concerning the legal process within the Commonwealth.

Activities

Study tours are arranged to see courts, penal institutions and other aspects of national legal systems in member countries. Triennial Conferences (Sydney, Australia (1991), Harare, Zimbabwe (1994), Cape Town, South Africa (1997), Edinburgh, Scotland (2000).

Training courses and workshops are held on plural legal systems, court administration, alternative dispute resolution methods, the judiciary and the media, human rights, women's rights and gender equality, sentencing skills. Training is undertaken under the auspices of a Director of Training.

Publications

- *Commonwealth Judicial Journal* (two issues per year)
- CMJA Newsletter (two issues per year)

COMMONWEALTH PARLIAMENTARY ASSOCIATION

Suite 700, Westminster House, 7 Millbank, London SW1P 3JA, UK

Tel: +44 (0) 171 799 1460

Fax: +44 (0) 171 222 6073

e-mail: hq.sec@comparlhq.org.uk

website: http://comparlhq.org.uk

Office bearers

President (1998–99): Hon Hector McClean, MP, Speaker of the House of Representatives, Trinidad and Tobago

Vice President (1998–99): Rt Hon Betty Boothroyd, MP, Speaker of the House of Commons, United Kingdom

Chairman of the executive Committee: Hon Billie Miller, MP (Barbados)

Secretary General: AR Donahoe, QC

Foundation

Founded in 1911, the CPA is an Association of Commonwealth parliamentarians who, irrespective of gender, race, religion or culture, are united by community of interest, respect for the rule of law and individual rights and freedoms, and by pursuit of the positive ideals of parliamentary democracy.

The Association is a charity registered under the laws of the United Kingdom.

Structure

The Commonwealth Parliamentary Association consists of 141 branches in the national, state, provincial or territorial parliaments in the countries of the Commonwealth. Conferences and general assemblies are held every year in different countries of the Commonwealth.

Aims

Its stated purpose is to promote knowledge and understanding of the constitutional, legislative, economic, social and cultural systems within a parliamentary democratic framework. It undertakes this mission with particular reference to the countries of the Commonwealth of Nations and to countries having close historical and parliamentary associations with it.

It provides the sole means of regular consultation among members of Commonwealth parliaments. It fosters co-operation and understanding among them and promotes the study and respect for parliament. Its role is endorsed by Commonwealth parliaments and heads of government.

Activities

It pursues these objectives by means of:

- Annual Commonwealth Parliamentary Conference, Regional Conferences and other symposiums
- Inter-parliamentary visits
- Parliamentary Seminars and Workshops
- Parliamentary Information and Reference Centre communications

Publications

Publications of the CPA include *The Parliamentarian* and two newsletters on CPA activities and on parliamentary and political events.

J   E:

H

2 0 JAN 2000	2 2 FEB 2000	2 2 NOV 2005
15 FEB 2000 CANCELLED	CANCELLED 2 6 APR 2001	
8 MAY 2000 CANCELLED		
2 3 MAY 2000 CANCELLED		
1 6 JAN 2001 CANCELLED		

This book is due to be returned not later than the date and
time stamped above. Fines are charged on overdue books

Limited

London • Sydney